Berlitz®

Boston

- A ✓ in the text denotes a highly recommended sight
- A complete A–Z of practical information starts on p.115
- Full mapping on cover flaps; Hotel and Blueprint maps in text

Berlitz Publishing Company, Inc.

Princeton Mexico City Dublin Eschborn Singapore

400 Alexander Park, Princeton, NJ, 08540 USA
9-13 Grosvenor St., London, W1X 9FB UK

Text: Fred Mawer
Layout: Media Content Marketing, Inc.
Photography: Jon Davison, Fred Mawer
Cartography: Visual Image

Although the publisher tries to insure the accuracy of all the information in this book, changes are inevitable and errors may result. The publisher cannot be responsible for any resulting loss, inconvenience, or injury. If you find an error in this guide, please let the editors know by writing to Berlitz Publishing Company, 400 Alexander Park, Princeton, NJ 08540-6306.

ISBN 2-8315-6290-2
Revised 1997 – Fourth Printing April 1999

Printed in Switzerland by Weber SA, Bienne
049/904 RP

CONTENTS

Fact Sheets

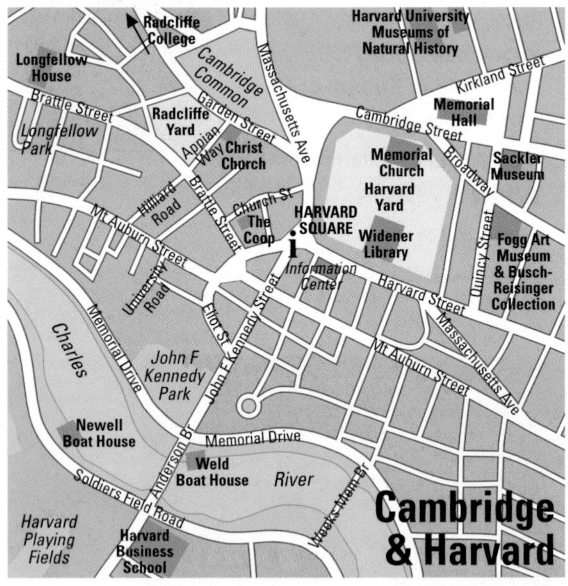
Cambridge & Harvard
Radcliffe College
Harvard University Museums of Natural History
Longfellow House
Cambridge Common
Massachusetts Ave
Kirkland Street
Brattle Street
Radcliffe Yard
Garden Street
Memorial Hall
Cambridge Street
Longfellow Park
Appian Way
Christ Church
Memorial Church
Broadway
Sackler Museum
Harvard Yard
Hilliard Road
Brattle Street
Church St
HARVARD SQUARE
Mt Auburn Street
The Coop
Widener Library
Quincy Street
Fogg Art Museum & Busch-Reisinger Collection
University Road
Information Center
Harvard Street
Memorial Drive
Eliot St
John F Kennedy Street
Massachusetts Ave
Charles
John F Kennedy Park
Mt Auburn Street
Newell Boat House
Anderson Br
Memorial Drive
Weld Boat House
River
Soldiers Field Road
Weeks Mem Br
Harvard Playing Fields
Harvard Business School

BOSTON

DO NOT
ENTER

BOSTON AND THE BOSTONIANS

From the Boston Tea Party to the Boston Massacre and the Midnight Ride of Paul Revere, around the world the capital of Massachusetts is synonymous with America's Revolutionary years. It was here that Britain's American colonies united in their struggle against colonial rule, and here the American War of Independence began.

Boston's prime glory is its past, and it is this rich history that first draws visitors. The city is one of America's most venerable, and an impressive number of its monuments and institutions are the country's first or oldest. This glorious heritage, however, is far from being Boston's sole attribute. Its skyscrapers may be smaller than, say, New York's, and the ancient buildings are less awesome than those of a European capital such as Rome, but you soon realize that what is so pleasing is the visual synthesis of old red brick and new glass towers set against winter snow, spring magnolia blossom, or the vibrant and kaleidoscopic colours of the fall. Within just a few square miles, boats and planes dash frenetically across the harbour, seagulls swoop round high-rise towers dwarfing the old colonial meeting houses below, and Victorian terraces line cobbled lanes.

This is a soothingly attractive concoction that now woos nearly five million tourists a year. Since the Puritans settled here in 1630, Boston has constantly proved a magnet for visitors. (Most Bostonians themselves were visitors once.) Nowadays they come in droves from around the world—particularly from Ireland and Italy—and neighbourhoods like the Irish South End or the Italian North End, with their ethnic sense of community, have managed to retain a strong identity.

Elegant Beacon Hill acquired its name from a beacon built on top of the hill in the 17th century.

It's difficult to imagine how small Boston is geographically, with a little over half a million inhabitants—although Greater Boston accounts for more than three million. The residents here often liken their neighbourhoods to villages (some might well be on first-name terms with the ticket issuer at the subway station). Many walk to work: distances are short, the sidewalks are safe, and the streets themselves are notoriously traffic-laden. "Shall we walk or do we have time to take a cab?," the joke goes. America's car culture just doesn't work in Boston, and the latest remedy is a $5 billion scheme—the Central Artery Third Harbor Tunnel Project, or "Big Dig"—which, when completed, will replace the ugly, elevated expressway which chews its way through town, with an underground highway. Another tunnel will also be buried under the harbour to the airport.

If truth be told, Bostonians rather like the traffic problem, since it reinforces their sense of individuality and solidarity in the face of adversity. In the same vein, saturation coverage of local sports by the media often overshadows stories of global significance. The city's very well-being seems wedded to the success of its various major league teams. When the Red Sox baseball team is on a winning streak, the headlines read "Ten games that shook the Hub," and columnists talk of a "Summer to smile about and enjoy." In every bar in town the television is tuned in when a home team is playing, and chat dries up for couples out for a romantic dinner.

Why the Hub? It was Oliver Wendell Holmes, author, professor of anatomy at Harvard University, and Chief Justice of the U.S. Supreme Court, who in 1858 encapsulated the city's sense of self-importance. Boston at that time was the country's intellectual and cultural powerhouse, known as the "Athens of America," and Holmes's declaration that its State House was "the hub of the solar system" soon became distorted to "Boston is the hub of the universe"—now the most quoted epithet on the city.

Today the Hub's intellectual legacy is reflected in its dozens of colleges—so many that no one seems to agree on an exact number—and the annual influx of hundreds of thousands of students. Culture and academia flourish disproportionately for a city this size. The Bostonian arts are allocated the most state funds per capita in the country, spawning a particularly rich spread of classical music and drama. Boston is a remarkably bookish place too, and some subway stops have a swaps system with racks to exchange reading material. If the hotel valet is being a little inattentive, it's probably because he's come to a crucial point in the novel he's reading.

Harvard and M.I.T. (Massachusetts Institute of Technology), two of America's most prestigious academic institutions, lie just "across the river," dominating the city of Cambridge. Visitors often think of Cambridge as an extension of the Hub, but it is actually an independent city, despite the fact that it's only a short subway ride away. Bostonians see their academic neighbours as head-in-the-clouds types, and because of the locals' left-of-centre tendencies, Cambridge is sometimes called the "People's Republic of Cambridge."

The recession at the end of the 1980s hit Boston and New England as hard as anywhere in the States. However, since the high-tech boom of the decade was more dramatic here than elsewhere, the fall was all the more painful; now, income growth is as slow and the cost of living as high as anywhere else in the country. Yet seeing this buzzing city at play, that can be hard to believe. Thanks largely to the student population, there's enough entertainment for a much bigger city. People corner you to tell you about their favourite restaurant or bar, and popular haunts are packed most nights. The long drawl of the upper-class "brahmin" set (sounding not unlike a contrived English accent) resonates in smart restaurants and tea rooms. Pints of Guinness and sing-alongs are the order of the day in the Irish pubs, and you would be hard pressed to find a seat in the city's best seafood restaurants.

However worldly-wise Boston might appear, it still has an appealing neighbourly quality. Enjoy its little quirks—a milkshake is a *frappé*, a soft drink a tonic—and it won't be long before you feel as much at home as the locals themselves.

Harvard Yard – the oldest and prettiest part of the famous Ivy League university.

A BRIEF HISTORY

Beginnings

The Algonquin Indians called the peninsula on which Boston stands Shawmut. In 1624, William Blackstone, a reclusive eccentric, became the first white inhabitant to live here. Legend has it that he settled on Shawmut with a good stock of books and a bull. In 1630, he invited some neighbours from Charlestown to join him on what is now Boston Common.

Like the pilgrims who had put down roots several years previously in Plymouth (see page 73), these neighbours were religious refugees from a little Lincolnshire town in England called Boston. They had fled from their homeland in order to avoid Anglicanism.

With John Winthrop leading them, the group—which was called the Massachusetts Bay Company—brought its own royal charter to the New World, a document which effectively authorized self-rule. The little community grew fast, and, with its excellent natural harbour, prospered as a trading port, exporting cod to Europe. In 1632 Boston became the capitol of the Massachusetts Bay Colony. The puritan ethical code in Boston meant that life was strict—too strict for Blackstone, who moved to Rhode Island.

A Question of Tax

Charles II came to the English throne in 1660, reinstating the Navigation Acts in that same year. These insisted that colonial trade be carried out solely with England, implementing a form of trade protectionism. Royal authority was further reinforced when the initial charter of the Massachusetts Bay Company was rescinded in 1684, and New England made a

Historical Landmarks

1630	Boston is founded by the Massachusetts Bay Company.
1635	Boston Latin, the country's first public school, is founded.
1636	Harvard University is founded.
1686	King James II revokes the Massachusetts Bay Company's original charter.
1765	The Stamp Act is introduced. Riots follow.
1767	The Townshend Acts are introduced. Riots follow.
1770	Five patriots killed in the Boston Massacre, 5 March.
1773	Boston Tea Party, 16 December.
1775	The War of American Independence begins on 19 April with skirmishes in Lexington and Concord.
1775	Great English losses at the Battle of Bunker Hill, 17 June.
1776	English troops retreat on Evacuation Day, 17 March.
1776	Signing of the Declaration of Independence in Philadelphia on 4 July.
1797	U.S.S. *Constitution* ("Old Ironsides") is launched.
1831	William Lloyd Garrison publishes the first edition of the abolitionist newspaper, *The Liberator*.
1857	Back Bay landfill project begins.
1872	Fire destroys 765 buildings in the Downtown area.
1875	Birth of the telephone: Alexander Graham Bell transmits speech sounds down a wire.
1879	Founding of the Christian Science movement by Mary Baker Eddy.
1897	The first subway in the country is opened, running from Boylston Street to Park Street.
1918	Red Sox win their last World Series title.
1919	A tidal wave of molasses in the North End kills 21.
1960	Massachusetts senator John F. Kennedy elected president of the United States.
1974	Buses are used to integrate predominantly black and white school districts; riots follow.
1983	Sitcom *Cheers* is first broadcast; greater renown follows.
1995	Boston Garden closes; Celtics, other teams move to FleetCenter

royal colony. Two years later, James II appointed the despotic Sir Edmund Andros as the royal governor of the Province of Massachusetts. His rule was short-lived, however, for when James II was deposed in 1689 in the Glorious Revolution, Andros was booted out, too.

In the first half of the 18th century, Boston continued to grow, becoming the largest city in North America. In addition, maritime trade flourished and many more wharves sprouted into the sea. Merchants started to compete with ministers as the community's leading figures, and the era was stamped by the erection of several public buildings, including Quincy Market Hall (on the Faneuil Hall Marketplace). The colony's prosperity didn't go unnoticed, so that by the time the coffers of the English treasury had been emptied in the Seven Years War with France (1756 to 1763), George III turned to the New World. He introduced a series of taxes, such as the Revenue or Sugar Act in 1764 (imposing duties on silk, wine, and sugar), and the Stamp Act in 1765, levying a tax on all publications. These measures prompted great dissent in Boston and caused crowds to riot.

The First Parish Church on the Green at Lexington, scene of the first battle on 19 April 1775.

As discontent grew, a group of protestors from all

walks of life was formed. Known as the Sons of Liberty, amongst its number were John Hancock, a wealthy dandy, Paul Revere, an artisan, and Samuel Adams, their leader, an idealist and Harvard graduate. Their rallying cry, "No taxation without representation," was echoed by the restless population. When the Townshend Acts were introduced in 1767, taxing lead, paper, and the colonists' favourite drink, tea, resentment rose further. Troops were sent in to occupy Boston and restore order, but still tension remained high, with many fracas between redcoated British soldiers and locals. On 5 March 1770, the Redcoats opened fire on an angry crowd, mortally wounding five. This error gave the cause its first martyrs, and the incident became renowned as the Boston Massacre.

In 1773, England, threatened by the commercial success of New England, sought to restrain its economic development with the Tea Act. In effect, this subsidized the East India Company's tea at the expense of colonial merchants. The colonials refused to pay the levied tax on tea, and after rounds of fruitless negotiations with the governor, on 16 December Samuel Adams spoke to the crowds at the Old South Meeting House: "Gentlemen, this meeting can do nothing more to save the country."

Colonial battle and drill re-enactments take place regularly in Lexington and Concord.

A thousand demonstrators went down to Griffin's

Wharf, where the Sons of Liberty boarded three vessels and dumped 342 chests of tea into the harbour. The Boston Tea Party was a clear act of defiance; the response from the British was to dissolve local government and close the harbour. The edicts declaring this move became known as the Intolerable Acts, and armed confrontation seemed inevitable.

War

The colonials began stockpiling arms and ammunitions. In April 1775, suspecting a horde of arms in Concord, 30 km (18 miles) northwest of Boston, General Thomas Gage, mili-

The Jack-of-All-Trades Patriot

Paul Revere is Boston's best loved son, due to his exploits on the night of 18 April 1775, immortalized in Henry Wadsworth Longfellow's *Paul Revere's Ride*:

Listen, my children, and you shall hear
Of the midnight ride of Paul Revere,
On the eighteenth of April, in Seventy-Five ...

He said to his friend, "If the British march
By land or sea from the town tonight,
Hang a lantern aloft in the belfry arch
Of the North Church tower as a signal light—
One, if by land, and two, if by sea...."

Revere often acted as a messenger for the Sons of Liberty and he was also a first-class propagandist for the cause by making provocative engravings, such as his famous one depicting the Boston Massacre. He was known primarily as a craftsman, however, and notably as a silversmith, but he also turned his hand to being a lieutenant-colonel of artillery, a copper roller, bell ringer, and dentist, while somehow finding time to sire 16 children from two wives. He died in 1818, aged 83.

tary governor of Massachusetts, planned its seizure. What took place next is the stuff of legends.

Paul Revere rode to Lexington where he met John Hancock and Samuel Adams, then continued on to Concord with Samuel Prescott and William Dawes. They were ambushed, but Prescott managed to complete the journey to warn the Minutemen (see page 70) of the English troops' arrival.

War broke out the next day, 19 April 1775. Redcoats killed colonial Minutemen on Lexington Green; there were casualties on both sides at North Bridge, and more fighting ensued as the English troops returned to Boston. On that first day, a total of 73 English and 49 colonists died. In the following weeks, colonial troops flooded into towns surrounding Boston to besiege the city.

The Hayes Memorial honors those who fought in the Revolutionary War.

On 17 June General Gage attempted to break the blockade in "The first great battle of the Revolution." It was fought at Breed's Hill in Charlestown, where the colonists had set up a redoubt, but due to a geographical confusion, it is now known as the Battle of Bunker Hill (see page 41).

The English underestimated the rebels' resolve, and though they officially won the battle, it was at a terrible cost, with more than

1,000 men killed or wounded. The siege of Boston continued through to the following year, under the command of General George Washington. On what is now called Evacuation Day (17 March 1776), the English troops, forced into retreat by Washington's artillery on Dorchester Heights, moved out of Boston. The war continued until 1783, but Boston itself was spared from further direct involvement.

Brahmins and Landfill

Maritime trade boomed after the Revolution, and industrial manufacturing began. Boston society focused on upper class merchants and industrialists. They had a reputation for their temperance, sobriety and high self-esteem, and consequently became known as "brahmins," after the Hindu caste that sets high moral standards.

The brahmins also valued culture, and the 19th century saw the founding of an array of cultural institutions. Boston became known as "The Athens of America," with writers like Henry Wadsworth Longfellow at the forefront of a renaissance in philosophical and literary thought. The city was a significant centre in the campaign for the abolition of slavery, as well as a stop-off point on the so-called "underground railroad" for smuggling slaves into Canada.

Charles Dickens visited in 1842, the same year that Longfellow's *Poems on Slavery* appeared. Dickens described Boston in his *American Notes*, remarking that "the air was so clear, the houses were so bright and gay; ... the gilded letters were so very golden; the bricks were so very red, the stone was so very white; ... the knobs and plates upon the street doors so very marvellously bright and twinkling." His favourable impression was thanks largely to the efforts of one man, the architect Charles Bulfinch (1763–1844). In starting a craze for Boston's distinctive, red-brick Georgian-style

Stars and Stripes — prosperity and freedom attracted thousands of immigrants right from the start.

buildings, he gave the city something of a facelift. Simultaneously, Boston was fast increasing in size.

Prior to the Revolution, the city's topography was far from impressive: a seemingly precarious peninsula on the end of a thin neck of land, with foul mud flats on either side. During the 1800s Boston's surface area increased threefold. The tops of the three original hills on which the city stood were lopped off, and the earth was used to extend the shoreline and cover over the marshes. Faneuil Hall Marketplace, the South End, Bay Village, and Back Bay are all the result of landfill projects. It took some 30 years, from 1857, to complete Back Bay, with trains importing wagonloads of gravel daily. The Victorian wonderland became a symbol of the city's prosperity and status.

Immigrants

Part of the reason for creating more space was the rapid increase in the city's population. Immigrants were pouring in from Ireland, leaving behind the Potato Famine (1845–50). They lived in poor conditions in tenements in the North and West End, and were often persecuted due to their Catholic faith. As they began to move out of the slums towards the end of the 19th century, new waves of immigrants began to arrive from Italy and eastern Europe in tens of thousands.

The Irish had a predilection for politics. Since 1885, when the first Irish mayor was appointed, few years have passed when the office has not been held by an Emerald Isle descendant. In the first half of this century, political life was dominated by John F. Fitzgerald ("Honey Fitz"), grandfather of the late President John Fitzgerald Kennedy, and James Michael Curley, who was mayor four times. Raised in poor neighbourhoods, the Irish were people's champions (even though Curley spent part of his fourth term in jail for fraud).

Renew or Recycle?

Ever since the Industrial Revolution, Boston has found itself increasingly overshadowed by New York in economic pre-eminence, and has suffered a gradual decline. In an attempt to revitalize the city, a massive urban renewal programme was undertaken in the 1960s, creating the Prudential Center in Back Bay and Government Center downtown. One of the most controversial renewal projects involved the destruction of the working-class West End, with neighbourhood streets sacrificed for apartment blocks.

A different philosophy has been adopted now. More than 7,000 city buildings are designated Historic Landmarks, and new uses have been found for old buildings: the former Natural History Museum is now a clothes store; Quincy Market has become Faneuil Hall Marketplace; and the naval yard and wharves have been transformed into offices and apartments. Post-war Boston was a commercial backwater. Then, in the 1980s, the city, with its many centres of academia, led the boom in high technology—a development which has since become known as the "Massachusetts Miracle."

WHERE TO GO

Boston is perfect for walking. The city is a delightfully compact place—you could stroll the length of the central districts in an hour and still not miss any of their utterly distinct neighbourhoods: the cobbled lanes on Beacon Hill, the jumble of streets among the Downtown skyscrapers, or the Victorian avenues of Back Bay are best appreciated on foot.

To get your bearings, start with the panoramic view from the John Hancock Observatory or take a fun trolley tour of the city centre and beyond—you can hop on and off at will.

If your time is limited, you may want just to stick to the Freedom Trail, a marked walking route that links the main historic sights. If you've got more time, it's better to explore the neighbourhoods separately. (Details of the main sights are given on pages 22–23.)

BOSTON COMMON AND BEACON HILL

Boston Common

The oldest public park in the United States is Boston's historical, spiritual, and geographical heart. Cows grazed here until banned in 1830. It has also always served as a great gathering place for people: in colonial times it was a military training camp and army base, and the city gallows once hung here. Another historical note is sounded by the copper-roofed **Park Street Station**, which, built in 1897, is the country's oldest subway station.

Mature trees and open space give the park an unmanicured, unembellished feel. There are no real sights to see, but an hour spent here introduces you to a cross-section of the city's inhabitants. Around the Visitor Information Booth on

The Massachusetts State House dates from 1798.

Tremont Street on the Common's east side, the tourist trolley companies tout their business while street artists and political activists provide entertainment. In the park proper, businesspeople stride on the way to or from work along the red brick paths, office workers tuck into lunch, the elderly sun themselves on park benches, students read, and tramps hang out by the bandstand and the Civil War Soldiers and Sailors Monument. On a hot day, kids play under the fountain at the **Frog Pond** (without frogs nowadays and once said to be a place for dunking witches). As evening approaches, tennis, volleyball, and softball get going. Thc lovely Public Garden nearby is described on page 49.

BOSTON HIGHLIGHTS

Listed below is a selection of "must see" sights and things to do for visitors who only have a short time in which to explore the city.

For Boston's best museums and galleries, see the Museums and Galleries box on page 54.

Exploring

The Freedom Trail: a red line running between the city's famous monuments—state buildings, churches, meeting houses, burial grounds—all recalling the hard-fought road to American Independence. (See page 25)

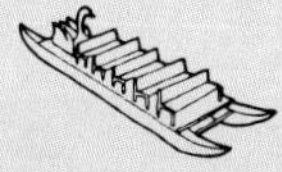

Public Garden: Boston's prettiest green patch, a leafy area complete with lawns, ornamental gardens, quirky sculptures and relaxing trips on the water on the Swan Boats during the summer. (See page 49)

Beacon Hill: red brick, slate-roofed houses on picturesque gas-lit cobbled streets of this historically protected district. (See pages 24–28)

The North End: discover the atmosphere and sights around the vivacious streets that offer a slice of Italy. (See pages 38–41)

Back Bay: the 19th-century landfill area that is now a fascinating grid of Victorian residential streets. (See pages 49–55)

Cambridge: arguably America's most famous centre of academia, where intellectual pursuits are complemented by trendy student hangouts around Harvard Square and the dignified beauty of Harvard Yard. (See pages 60–68)

Views

John Hancock Observatory: New England's tallest building offers an unequalled view over Boston. (See page 50)

Boston Harbor trip: for splendid views across the water of the city's skyscrapers. (See pages 46–47)

Water Works

Whale watching: Boston's biggest thrill; sailing the ocean in search of humpback, fin and minke whales. Boat trips almost always (but never completely) guarantee a sighting of one of these magnificent creatures. (See pages 47–49)

Shopping

Faneuil Hall Marketplace: one of Boston's most popular attractions: a touristy but fun mall in a highly successful conversion of traditional 18th-century market buildings. (See pages 33–34)

Newbury Street: Boston's trendiest shops, in Back Bay, for art, antiques, and just about anything avant-garde. (See page 53)

Filene's Basement: lowest prices in the famous bargain store; keep an eye open for discounted discounts advertised in local papers. (See page 37)

Entertainment

Red Sox game: a must for baseball afficionados and newcomers alike; don't miss a game—it could even be the one that wins the World Series. The *Celtics* (basketball), *Bruins* (ice hockey) and the *Patriots* (American football) also play in the Boston area. (See page 57 and 91)

Boston Pops: popular classical concerts in the city that is second only to New York for classical music; performed by the Boston Symphony Orchestra—a city institution—in May, June, and on 4 July. (See page 86)

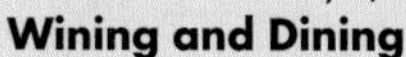

Wining and Dining

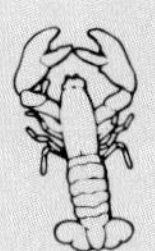

Seafood extravaganza: try a branch of the Legal Sea Foods restaurant—delicious specialities straight from the Atlantic. (See page 96)

Café life: at its best on Hanover Street in the North End or outdoor cafés on Newbury Street. (See page 38 and 53)

Irish pubs: meet the locals—try the Black Rose by Faneuil Hall Marketplace. (See page 90)

The State House

Shining above the trees in the north corner of the Common is the gold-leaf dome of Charles Bulfinch's hilltop **Massachusetts State House**. The building's fine neoclassical façade has columns and brick arches. It has been greatly expanded since it was built in 1798, but fortunately to little detrimental effect. Office workers bustle in and out in time with the candid, striding statue of John F. Kennedy in front of the building's western flank.

Inside, on the ground floor, statues and murals of key figures and events in the history of Massachusetts (and therefore that of the United States) line a series of palatial rooms faced with marble of varying hues. Upstairs, go into the superb mahogany-panelled, oval-shaped House of Representatives, where you will find the famous pine Sacred Cod hanging, symbol of the fishing industry's importance to the state. Also up here is the elegantly proportioned, domed Senate Chamber. Continuing around the corner, ignore the policeman to sneak a look at the secretary, hard at work in the Governor's waiting room.

Red-bricks and black shutters—the hallmarks of Beacon Hill.

Beacon Hill

Boston's most "civilized" residential neighbourhood really feels like a sleepy old village, well insulated from much of the traffic and vulgarity of the 20th century. The building of the State

House made the district desirable, while the first half of the 19th century saw the advent of red brick houses—some designed by Charles Bulfinch—for wealthy brahmin families.

Today, little seems to have changed: Successive generations of families have worked hard to preserve the streets and houses of this area, which has now been officially designated an historic district. Strains of classical music waft

Follow the Red Brick Line

The **Freedom Trail** wiggles through central Boston, linking 16 colonial and revolutionary sights. There's a line of red bricks or paint to follow, so you don't need to pore over a map.

The trail begins officially at the Visitors Information Booth on Tremont Street and runs as far as the Bunker Hill Monument in Charlestown, but with no chronology to the sights, you can stop or start, or even do it in reverse, without losing anything.

It's supposed to be just 4 km (2½ miles) end to end, but with all its twist and turns, it feels longer. Don't attempt to do it all at once; besides, if you start at Boston Common, you'll be pushed to reach the U.S.S. *Constitution* in Charlestown before it shuts.

All but two of the sights (Old South Meeting House and Paul Revere House) are free. For an abbreviated tour, try stopping only at the following: the Granary Burial Ground, Old South Meeting House (detour to Boston Tea Party Ship and Museum), Faneuil Hall, Paul Revere House, Old North Church, U.S.S. *Constitution*, Bunker Hill Monument. The trail is managed by Boston National Historic Park: see page 114 for tours.

We also recommend that you spend plenty of time well away from the Freedom Trail: Boston and Cambridge have lots to offer in addition to their significant historical legacy.

A flower market adds local colour.

from ivy-covered buildings with black shutters and wrought iron railings. Bootscrapers stand outside the door on the front steps and geraniums overflow from window boxes. Leafy streets—could they be otherwise with names like Walnut, Cedar, and Willow?—dapple the sunlight on brick-lined pavements.

Charles Street serves as the community's main street and as a magnet for serious antique collectors. Carefully scrolled wooden placards advertise antique shops, estate agents, and hardware stores, as well as an impressive selection of high-class cafés and restaurants.

The most rewarding parts of Beacon Hill lie to the hilly east of Charles Street, where the quiet residential streets of the North Slope can be found between Pinckney and Cambridge streets. Head down Joy Street to the **African Meeting House** (see page 27) and to 141 Cambridge Street for the **Harrison Gray Otis House** (guided tours Tuesday–Friday, noon–5:00 P.M.; Saturday, 10:00 A.M.–5:00 P.M.). The rooms of this fine Federal-style Bulfinch house have been lovingly restored to the style of the early 19th century, when they were occupied by two "yuppies" of the time, Otis and his wife.

For the quintessential, old-monied Beacon Hill, however, you need to head for the South Slope, between Pinckney and Beacon streets. You can't have a smarter address in Boston than one of the two stretches of classic, bow-fronted façades

The Black Heritage Trail

Massachusetts declared slavery illegal in 1783. In subsequent years, many blacks settled in the North End and Beacon Hill. An interesting tour connects landmarks of Boston's 19th-century African-American community on Beacon Hill. Follow it with the aid of the widely available leaflet, or be guided by a National Park ranger (telephone 742-5415 for departure times).

Tours leave from the ROBERT GOULD SHAW AND 54TH REGIMENT MEMORIAL, opposite the State House on Beacon Street. It honours both the first black regiment and those who died in a famous Civil War battle (as depicted in the film *Glory*). These black soldiers served without pay until granted a salary equal to their white counterparts. The reverse of the memorial movingly praises them and pays tribute to their white officers for "casting their lot with men of a despised colour."

The tour's other focal point is the AFRICAN MEETING HOUSE. The oldest black church in the U.S., built with black hands in 1806, it stands opposite the pretty clapboard houses of Smith Court, off Joy Street. During the 19th century it became a political and abolitionist centre—the New England Anti-Slavery Society was founded here in 1832—earning the nickname Black Faneuil Hall. In the downstairs area, The Museum of Afro-American History holds a collection of historic pamphlets and works by contemporary black artists. Upstairs, the intimate galleried meeting room has been beautifully restored.

in sloping **Louisburg Square**. **Nichols House** (55 Mount Vernon Street; open for guided tours Tuesday–Saturday, noon–5:00 P.M., May–October; Monday, Wednesday, and Friday, 12:15 P.M.–4:15 P.M., February–April and November–December), one of the cosiest-looking houses, built by Bulfinch, offers an opportunity to peruse the interior of a brahmin home. The rooms are exactly as they were when the owner died in 1960, fitted out entirely with pre-Victorian furniture. Don't forget **Acorn Street**—the prettiest of them all—a cobbled lane so narrow that cars can't park here to spoil a photographer's picture.

A Sitcom Shrine

Boston's top single attraction, on Beacon Street opposite the Public Garden, is properly called the Bull and Finch—a wordplay on the city's best-known architect—but is better known as Cheers. It was a normal neighbourhood hangout until a couple of Hollywood producers popped in more than a decade ago and decided to make what turned out to be a fantastically successful sitcom series based on the bar. Long-time regulars speak of now and BC – "Before Cheers." What you see on television is very different from the actual bar, though some features such as the brick walls and Tiffany lamps have been copied in the studio set. It's also incredibly crowded, mostly with tourists. Thursdays at 9pm is the busiest time of all, when *Cheers* repeats are shown on TV. The quietest time to visit is about 4 P.M.

The Esplanade

If you explore westwards from Charles Street, and go through the Flats—a landfill area of Beacon Hill—you come to the Esplanade, a long narrow park along the Charles River. This is where Bostonians exercise to their heart's content, working up a sweat either jogging, walking, cycling, or rollerblading. If it's a sunny day, you'll also come across painters and sunbathers, the former striving to encapsulate on canvas the constantly changing scene of the river and small sailboats. The much-loved **Boston Pops Orchestra** performs in the Art Deco Hatch Memorial Shell during July; the 4th of July performance is a knockout (see page 86).

DOWNTOWN

This is Boston's commercial and financial heart, but it's not an homogenous district: within the confines of the austere Government Center and the lively Faneuil Hall Marketplace to the north, and colourful Chinatown to the south, lie gaudy glass skyscrapers, Art Deco towers, and old-fashioned department stores. Red brick historic relics—survivors of a great fire in 1872—remind you that 200 years ago this condensed maze of narrow streets was nothing more than rutted, muddy lanes.

The Old Amongst the New

A chunk of the Freedom Trail winds through the Downtown area, from the northeast corner of Boston Common.

Park Street Church stands on a site nicknamed Brimstone Corner (some say for the fiery sermons of the church's congregationalist preachers, others for the fact that gunpowder was kept in its basement during the 1812 War). Built on the site of a granary in 1809, this Georgian Church's most beautiful feature is the 66-meter (217-foot) tall triple-tiered steeple, based on a Christopher Wren design.

A peaceful oasis lies behind here off busy Tremont Street. The **Granary Burying Ground** is cram-packed with the bones of many heroes of the Revolutionary period: John Hancock, Paul Revere, Samuel Adams, James Otis, the victims of the Boston Massacre. A map near the entrance locates the gravestones of the famous. As in all Boston's old graveyards, many headstones are delicately inscribed with both a skull and crossbones and winged death's head motifs. Headstones have been moved over the years to accommodate newcomers and the lawnmower, with the result that they do not mark accurately where remains actually lie; furthermore, a couple of dozen bodies may be interred under each stone.

Continue northwards along Tremont Street to the squat, granite **King's Chapel** (Tuesday–Saturday, 10:00 A.M.–2:00 P.M.). The first Anglican place of worship in Boston, it stands on land pinched from the burial ground next door: the Puritans refused to sell any land that would be used for the benefit of a religion they had left England to avoid. The surprisingly elaborate interior has lavishly upholstered pews—in particular the Governor's—in boxes designed to prevent worshippers from feeling the draughts. Also here is the oldest continually used pulpit in the U.S.

Next door is **King's Chapel Burial Ground**, the city's oldest. Here lie William Dawes, the lesser-known messenger of the midnight ride to Lexington (see page 16), and John Winthrop, the colony's first governor.

Follow the red brick line down School Street, which is named after Boston Public Latin School. Founded in 1635 and the oldest school in the U.S., it is also commemorated by a mosaic outside the Old City Hall, where it first stood. (It's now in the Fenway; students there still have to study Latin.) Benjamin Franklin was an early pupil, and you can see his statue here. The Old City Hall has been superseded by the

Government Center, and is now home to a recommended French restaurant.

Ho Chi Minh once worked in the kitchens and Malcolm X as a waiter in the Omni Parker House, back on the corner of Tremont Street. It is the oldest continually operating hotel in the country.

Boston's old food halls are now a lively marketplace.

At the end of School Street, the lovely red brick building with a "gambrel" roof—wide, sloping at two angles—dates from the early 1700s. It's now the **Globe Corner Bookstore**. In the 19th century, it was called the Old Corner Bookstore, and it was from here that the first works of such literary giants such as Emerson, Longfellow, and Dickens were sold.

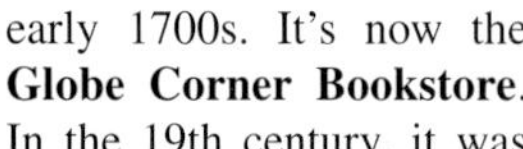

Diagonally opposite, across the way on Washington Street, the monumental tower blocks dwarf the tapering spire of the **Old South Meeting House**. Here a massive crowd rallied against the tea tax on the fateful day, 16 December 1773, and Samuel Adams gave the signal that allowed the Boston Tea Party to begin (see page 14). During the siege of Boston, the English desecrated the church, but, needless to say, it has since been carefully restored. It's one of the best stops on the Freedom Trail: The historic appearance of the balconied hall has been preserved completely, while semi-transparent life-size characters and the tea tax debate relayed on headphones enhance the atmosphere fur-

Huguenot merchant Peter Faneuil would be delighted with the success of his market today.

ther. Well-positioned boards give plenty of information.

If you continue up Washington Street, you'll soon find the Downtown shopping area (see page 83), from where the Freedom Trail doubles back on itself to the **Old State House**, a chunky brick building with a wedding cake belltower. This was the centre of political life in Colonial times and the State Capitol after the Revolution. From the balcony of the Council Chamber on the first floor, the American Declaration of Independence was read on 18 July 1776. The gold lion and silver unicorn above, symbols of the British crown, are replicas of originals that were destroyed that same day. Inside, displays and mementos detail Boston's Revolutionary history, while forceful exhibitions bring to life more recent periods of the city's past.

It's easy to miss the circle of stones in a traffic island in front of the Old State House. These indicate the site of the so-called **Boston Massacre** on 5 March 1770, when British troops opened fire on an angry crowd, killing five. One result of the incident was that anti-British propagandists gained much mileage, as is illustrated by Paul Revere's famous engraving of the event.

Faneuil Hall Marketplace

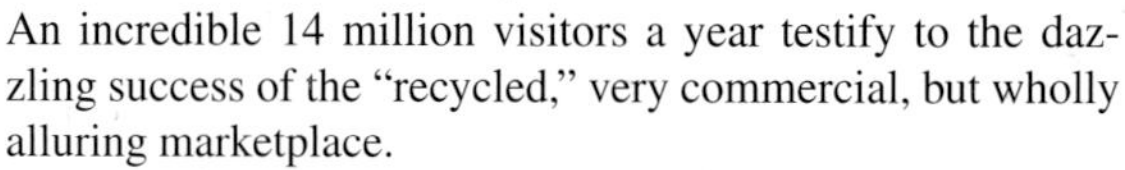

An incredible 14 million visitors a year testify to the dazzling success of the "recycled," very commercial, but wholly alluring marketplace.

Named after its benefactor, the Huguenot merchant Peter Faneuil (pronounced *fannel*, *fan'l* or *funnel*), **Faneuil Hall** dates back to 1742. Its most famous decoration is a gleaming grasshopper weathervane atop the belltower, long a symbol of the city. By Bulfinch's time the hall had become too small, so in 1806 he enlarged it in all directions. The interior houses a ground-floor market area, but the interest lies upstairs in the lovely galleried meeting hall, which is enclosed by tiers of white columns and decorated with the paintings of many famous Americans. All the weighty issues that were thrashed out here in Revolutionary times—debates on unfair taxes and rousing speeches by Samuel Adams and others—earned the hall the title of "The Cradle of Liberty." Ever since, it has been a political forum—a meeting-place, for example, for rallies for the abolition of slavery and for women's rights—and today many contemporary political campaigns are launched here. The now ceremonial Ancient and Honorable Artillery Company of Massachusetts—the oldest militia in the United States, founded in 1637—has its museum here in the attic (open Monday–Friday, 10:00 A.M.–4:00 P.M.). On display is a collection of military paraphernalia including flags, muskets, and so forth.

The long, low buildings that back on to Faneuil Hall are home to **Quincy North and South Markets**. When built in 1826, they were actually at the harbour's edge. Older Bostonians recall the stench of rancid meat emanating from them on a hot summer's day. Then in the 1970s a colossal gentrification programme won the day. Rather than demolish the ailing area, it was decided to turn the old food markets into a vast indoor and outdoor mall to be called Faneuil Hall Marketplace. Today, canvas stalls and café parasols enliven the brick and granite buildings. Throngs of tourists and locals enjoy the street performers and browse in the boutiques, and at lunch time ravenous hordes descend on the delectable fast-food emporium in the central Quincy Market: snackers with a slice of pizza, a cup of chowder, or a bagel cover every inch of sidewalk. In the evening, the area reverberates with busy restaurants, bars, and live jazz.

One establishment has remained from the market's earliest days: join the communal tables at **Durgin Park** restaurant, try the wholesome Yankee cooking, and pit your wits against the no-nonsense waitresses.

Government Center

Perhaps the best that can be said for Government Center is that its awfulness might have contributed to the enlightened rescue of adjacent Faneuil Hall Marketplace. Due to a 1960s urban renewal plan, the seedy but lively Scollay Square was replaced with soulless spaces and monolithic buildings, like City Hall Plaza and City Hall—little less than a horrible concrete monster on legs. The complex has been enlivened somewhat with the recent addition of a garden with terraces, pools, and niches where music is performed.

The only permanent point of interest can be found in the form of the outsize **Steaming Kettle** on the south side of the square above the door of the eponymous coffee shop. Commissioned by the Oriental Tea Company in 1873, it is an appropriate landmark for a city so closely linked to tea. Its capacity is printed on its side: 227 gallons, 2 quarts, 1 pint, 3 gills (some 868 litres).

Blackstone Block

A neon sign beckons northeast of the plaza, advertising the oldest restaurant in the United States, the **Union Oyster House**. The building dates from 1713, the restaurant from 1826. Even if you don't intend to eat there, peer in the window at the oysters and clams being shucked at the raw bar (the establishment gets through as many as 4,000 oysters on a busy day).

The restaurant stands in the Blackstone Block, a tiny patch of old, red brick commercial buildings divided by narrow alleys that has somehow survived over the years. Look out for the Boston Stone set in the wall of a gift shop on Marshall Street. It was formerly used for grinding paint from pigments, but was put here in 1737 as, some say, a distance marker.

Don't miss the colourful fruit and vegetable market that takes place at the Haymarket, just behind Blackstone Block, on Friday and Saturday.

Skyscrapers and Shops

Downtown Boston does not have any great, singular monuments to conspicuous excess: by New York or Chicago stan-

Catching up on stocks and shares or checking out what is playing? Have a seat at Faneuil Hall Marketplace.

dards its high-rise district is understated. Yet as a group, these buildings still manage to impress, particularly if viewed from the harbour (see page 46).

To get a closer look at them, head downtown on a weekday morning or afternoon, when people in suits bustle purposefully from A to B. **State Street** was once the main route from the wharves to the Old State House. It now symbolizes the 1980s boom, notably in the showy glass tower of the stock exchange building (53 Exchange Place) and its monumental marble staircase in the foyer, and in the ostentatious marble atrium foyer of number 75. Off the harbour end of State Street is the bizarre **Custom House Tower**: a 19th-century, Greek Revival temple base to which was added Boston's first skyscraper in 1917. The building was transformed yet again in 1997, when much of it was converted to time-share vacation units.

For a good view of some of Downtown's new and not-so-new buildings, go to the green triangle of Post Office Square.

The Financial District's crop of skyscrapers is best appreciated from Boston Harbor.

Stepped sides and Art Deco style wall decorations make the **New England Telephone Building** on the southern edge of the square one of the most arresting. The lobby celebrates the proletarian history of the telephone with a 360-degree mural. You can also pop in to a little room off the lobby that reproduces the attic room of Alexander Bell from nearby Court Street. It was from there that he first transmitted sounds electrically over a wire in 1875 (open Monday–Friday, 8:30 A.M.–5:00 P.M.).

The city's malls now outshine the shopping district of **Downtown Crossing** (around the crossroads of Washington, Summer, and Winter streets), but here you'll discover long-established department stores like Jordan Marsh and Filene's Basement. It's hard to imagine the pedestrianized Washington Street joining the Old State House south to the neck of the Shawmut peninsula before the landfills. A few quaint stores are hidden down side alleys, as is the *fin-de-siècle* Locke-Ober (in Winter Place), which has served traditional dishes to the well-heeled business set for over a century.

Discount record stores peter out into porn shops and seedy bars at the south end of Washington Street: this is the **Combat Zone**, an area best avoided at night.

The Basement

Not to be mixed up with Filene's, the smart department store upstairs, Filene's Basement is the oldest discount store in the country. It mainly sells clothes, by no means all unfashionable, as testified by the racks of stylish overcoats, suits and designer-label collections. Prices start low and can be marked down by a further 75 percent. After 35 days, goods are given away to charity. Look out for newspaper advertisements for sale dates and prepare for a scuffle over the best items. Happy hunting!

There are said to be over 50 restaurants in **Chinatown**, the crowded blocks bordered by Washington, Kneeland, and Essex streets and the Expressway. Even if you don't intend to eat there (dining is generally inexpensive and possible until the early hours of the morning—unique in Boston), it's worth experiencing the sights and smells of this culturally intact community. Chinese jewellers, groceries, bakers, and clothes shops nestle among the pagoda-topped telephone boxes and below the big neon signs advertising dim sum and cocktails.

THE NORTH END

The Atmosphere

"FBI—Full Blooded Italian" and "Life's too short not to be Italian" shout out T-shirts all around Boston's most entrancing neighbourhood. Here, restaurants are loudly decked out with garish murals announcing the likes of "*Mangia calimari*" or "50 different ways to enjoy pasta." Cafés, with big *espresso* machines sitting in the windows, each claim to serve the "best tiramisu."

These are good times for the city's oldest district. From its well-to-do beginnings in colonial days, it became an overpopulated harbourside slum in the 19th century as immigrants—Irish, Jewish, and Portuguese—came and moved on once they had found their feet. The Italians took hold in the 1920s and made the area the lovable, close-knit community it is today: ladies in aprons camp out in deckchairs in the evenings.

Hop on to the Freedom Trail and head to **Hanover Street**, the North End's commercial backbone. If you think that the long line of cafés and restaurants is just for tourists, then come in the morning and drink an *espresso* with the locals—characters indeed.

On weekend evenings the older generation is replaced by the liqueur and *gelati* crowd, and no place more so than at 296, the cavernous Caffè Vittoria. Examine the walls for splendid black and white portraits of the area.

The other atmospheric thoroughfare is **Salem Street**, just north of Hanover, where you'll find wonderful backstreet delicatessens that smell of fresh pasta and salami,

Italian *feste*

Most summer weekends, some part of the North End comes alive with revels that wouldn't look out of place in a Sicilian or Tuscan square. Indeed, the cause for such festivities is the celebration of saints local to the North Enders' villages, back in Italy. Tinsel and lights are hung across the street and in the evenings a traditional brass band plays the favourite tunes. Matronly Italian mamas collect raffle tickets and pin the proceeds on drapes hanging from the saint's statue, while kids bounce basketballs and throw darts in fairground stalls. Other stalls sell calzone, mozzarella sticks, homemade meatballs and fried calamari. Sunday is the day of the big procession, when the statue is walked around the neighbourhood on men's shoulders while bystanders throw confetti and balloons.

newsagents selling *Corriere della Sera* and *La Gazzetta dello Sport*, and Bova, a first-rate, 24-hour bakery at 134, bursting with delectable cakes.

The Sights

The twee and wooden-slatted **Paul Revere House** on pretty North Square is the oldest building in Boston. Built a little under a century before America's best known patriot acquired it in 1770, it looks and feels like a big cottage, with creaky stairs and beams. Both the kitchen and living room downstairs are furnished with 17th-century pieces, while the two bedrooms upstairs contain furniture that once actually belonged to Revere.

Nathaniel Hichborn used to be his cousin Paul's next-door neighbour when living in what is now the **Pierce-Hichborn House**, one of the city's earliest brick buildings, built in Georgian style. On most days, there are two guided tours (details available from the Paul Revere House; telephone 523-1676 for details).

Back on Hanover Street is **St. Stephen's Church**, Boston's only remaining Bulfinch church. It looks down what the locals call the Prado, officially known as **Paul Revere Mall**. The equestrian statue of Paul Revere, set against the steeple of Old North Church rising out of the foliage, is one of the most photographed sights in the city. Locals chat on the stone benches of the promenade, while tourists inspect the bronze plaques on the brick walls which pay tribute to the North End's famous sons.

Not only is the **Old North Church** (properly known as Christ Church) the city's oldest, it is also the most famous and beautiful. Lit up at night, its landmark steeple (actually rebuilt in 1955) is visible from far away in Downtown. It was here that on 18 April 1775 sexton Robert Newman, following Paul Revere's orders, lit two lanterns ("one, if by land, and two, if by sea") to warn that the British were approaching by water, a practice that Revere's and Newman's descendants carry out on the eve of Patriot's Day each year (see page 89). The bright white, galleried interior looks much as it always has, with beautiful high box pews owned by the parishioners (see the names on the brass plaques) and impressive shiny brass chandeliers.

The last Freedom Trail stop in the North End is **Copp's Hill Burying Ground**, which is the prettiest of Boston's old cemeteries, but has no graves of famous people. At the Battle of Bunker Hill (see page 16), the English fired their cannons on Charlestown from here—you can still see the chips on the slate gravestones which the Redcoats used for target practice at that time.

Head west down Commercial and Causeway streets, and you will soon come to North Station and the site of **Boston Garden**, the beloved arena for Bruins ice hockey and Celtics basketball teams until 1995. It has been replaced by FleetCenter (telephone 624-1000 for information on events).

CHARLESTOWN

Charlestown was founded in 1629, one year earlier than the founding of Boston. It was virtually demolished in the Battle of Bunker Hill, and nowadays the town houses of wood and brick which were rebuilt on its slopes (now the preserve of the middle classes) constitute a very pleasant stroll. The 67-meter (220-foot) tall tapering granite obelisk forms the **Bunker Hill Monument** and commemorates the first battle of the Revolution, on 17 June 1775—a hollow victory for the British who lost many men. It actually stands on Breed's Hill, the site of the colonial redoubt in the battle. At its base is a swashbuckling statue of the American Colonel Prescott, who gave the famous order: "Don't fire 'til you see the whites of their eyes." There are informative models depicting the battle's progress as well as hourly musket-firing demonstrations. If you climb the 294 spiraling steps to the top, you may well be disappointed to find that it is enclosed, but the views are still great. The Bunker Hill Pavilion, situated between the Naval Yard and Charlestown Bridge, re-enacts the battle in a fiery, 30-minute "multi-media spectacular."

The main attraction in the Charlestown Navy Yard at the bottom of the hill is the venerable **U.S.S. *Constitution***. Better known as "Old Ironsides" for the fact that her oak timbers caused cannonballs to bounce off her sides, she is the oldest commissioned warship in the world, originally launched in 1797. The guides are enlisted sailors who sleep on board; even if she is still in dry dock without her guns, masts, and rigging and you can only visit her decks, they still provide an enjoyable tour (you may well have to wait in line for a tour in summer). Every 4th of July she is taken out to sea and put on show in a turnaround cruise. The excellent **Constitution Museum** brings to life the famous victories in which she was involved, as well as living conditions on board. There's also the

Crew members of the* U.S.S. *Constitution ("Old Ironsides") give guided tours of their boat.

World War II destroyer **U.S.S. *Cassin Young*** to visit, not to mention guided tours of the Naval Yard conducted by the park rangers. The yard was actually sold off in 1974 and has largely been converted into private offices.

You can get yourself to Charlestown: along the Freedom Trail (roughly a 15-minute walk from Copp's Hill to the Naval Yard); by the MBTA's Orange Line to Community College (10 minutes to Bunker Hill Monument); or by taking the water shuttle from Long Wharf.

Waterfront

Wharves poke out of Downtown and the North End into Boston Harbor like spines on a hedgehog. There was a time when Boston's port was the second busiest in the United States, with clippers sailing in and out of the harbour. After a long period of decline, renovation similar to that at Faneuil Hall Marketplace (see page 33) has transformed the granite warehouses into apartments, restaurants, offices, and hotels, while sleek pleasure cruisers have since taken the place of sailing ships. The best part of a stroll along the waterfront is enjoying the myriad craft in the harbour and the exciting, even alarming, sight of aircraft descending from the sky over the water on the approach run into Logan Airport.

Before landfill projects took place, the start of **Long Wharf** was near the Old State House. Cruise companies organize sightseeing and whale-watch trips along the quay. Its tip offers panoramic views.

On Central Wharf, the **New England Aquarium** is as informative as any you're likely to come across. A blue penumbra creates the sense of being underwater. Its centrepiece is a giant tank filled with sharks, sea turtles, coral, and all sorts of fish, which you circle on an escalating ramp. Other aquaria around the sides illustrate several habitats: a salt marsh, a mangrove swamp, or the New England seashore, where you can handle crabs and starfish. At the "Northern Waters of the World" you can see live octopuses, lobsters, and scallops, as well as dolphin and sea-lion shows several times daily. A new wing, scheduled to open in early 1998, will increase the size of the aquarium by more than a third.

Continuing south, you come to the superb **Rowes Wharf**, a modern design set around a colossal domed archway. You could have a bite to eat or a cup of tea in the luxurious but informal Boston Harbor Hotel or dine aboard the cruise ships that depart from the marina.

Fort Point Channel divides Downtown from South Boston (confusingly to the east). The rigging of *Beaver II*, by one of the rusty bridges across the channel, looks en-

Penguins feel quite at home in the watery world of the New England Aquarium.

tirely out of place in the midst of so much modernity. It was, in fact, built in 1973 in Denmark and sailed across the Atlantic in time for the 200th anniversary of the Boston Tea Party. The brig is a copy of one of the three ships on which the patriots, dressed as Indians, wasted 342 chests of tea on 16 December 1773 (see page 14). The **Boston Tea Party Ship and Museum** invites you to explore the decks and hold of *Beaver II* and even toss a roped bail of tea over the side. A museum on the small, adjacent pier relays the incident's background. The shop does a brisk trade in tea towels, mugs, and, of course, packets of the precious leaves.

Two superb museums await you across Fort Point Channel. A giant milk bottle outside hints at what's here: the **Children's Museum** manages to be both a vast playground and a stimulating learning centre. The buzz words here are "hands on": there are strange sculptures to climb over, bubbles to make, and hopscotch to play in Chinese and Italian in the Kid's Bridge—an introduction to Boston's multiculturalism. The most original part of the museum is an entire Japanese house, with bathroom, kitchen, and authentic smell, and Teen Toyko, where you can ride the subway and take up the Sumo Challenge.

Next door the wholly absorbing **Computer Museum** appeals to all levels of computer literacy. A walk through the innards of a desktop computer 50 times larger than life demonstrates exactly how the hardware works, while a video explains how an idea in the human mind can end up as a software programme. You can take the opportunity to compose music, plan a wedding, or design a car on endless interactive games. Advanced computers upstairs draw graphics, and smart machines—more commonly known as robots—show off

Having a whale of a time! The sight of one of these massive creatures is one you won't forget.

their skills. An exhaustive trawl through the history of the computer shows how technology has developed over the years, up to today.

TAKING TO THE WATER

On a fine day, a boat trip in Boston Harbor is idyllic. The rectangular, tubular, and pyramid shapes of the downtown skyscrapers look quite magnificent. The water is alive with yachts, speedboats, tugs, and fishing craft, while a constant stream of jets descends on to the waterside runways of one of the world's busiest airports.

Harbor Islands

As you reach the outer harbour, the urban scenery fades, replaced by the jumble of indecipherable green lumps of some 30 tiny islands. Gulls hover over lobster pots then perch on rocky outcrops; floating channel markers and small lighthouses abound.

There's not that much to do or see on the seven islands that make up the largely uninhabited Boston Harbor Islands

State Park, but an afternoon spent there offers a welcome respite from urban excitement. (Save for the noise of planes overhead, the islands are delightfully peaceful—a far cry from the bright lights of the city whose distant skyline sits prettily on the horizon.)

The islands are perfect for gentle strolls, picnics, and bird-watching. From May to mid-October, the Bay State Cruise Company (telephone 723-7800) runs a ferry from Long Wharf to **Georges Island**, the core of the group. This is the one island that sometimes has fresh water, and there's even a snack bar there. Most of it is taken up by Fort Warren, a 19th-century star-shaped fortress in which confederate prisoners were incarcerated at the time of the Civil War. It's an atmospheric and spooky place, with old gun emplacements, lookout posts, and chilly alleys.

You can also visit five other islands—Peddocks, Lovells, Bumpkin, Gallops, and Grape—on a free water-shuttle service from Georges Island from July to Labor Day. Lovells is the only island with a designated swimming area. For details on camping, see page 107.

Looking for Leviathans

One of the most exciting experiences you can have in Boston is whale-watching. From April through to October, literally dozens of sightseeing craft from Boston and other ports scattered along the New England coast head out to an area known as Stellwagen Bank, where whales stock up in the plankton and fish-filled waters before migrating to the warmer Caribbean climes. If you sail from Gloucester and Provincetown, the most handy points of departure, you will spend less time getting there and more time actually looking for whales. For details of sightseeing and whale-watching trips, see page 115.

Humpbacks are most commonly spotted, but you might also come across the larger fin whales (which measure up to 24 meters (80 feet) in length—the second biggest species after blue whales) and swift, 9-meter (30-foot) long minkes. You can be almost sure to get at least some glimpse of a whale. In fact, on a good day you may see as many as forty. (You are more likely to see greater numbers if the weather is poor.)

When the commentator—who is usually a well-qualified naturalist—makes a sighting, everyone rushes to one side of the boat, causing it to lurch suddenly. The boat heads off hopefully towards the telltale sign of the spume of water, and then suddenly, in the murky green of the depths below, there it is: a silvery flank virtually underneath the boat. A glimpse of an arched back, the nonchalant flick of a V-shaped tail, or fluke, and it's gone. If you are very lucky, you may see the rare spectacle of a whale breaching, heaving its entire body out of the

Mrs. Mallard leads the line of ducks celebrating the popular children's tale.

water. At times, it seems as if the whales themselves are doing the watching, when they approach the boats on their own, swim underneath them, and stare up at the tourists.

BACK BAY

In the middle of the 19th century, Boston ended at Boston Common and Back Bay was just a polluted tidal flat. In the space of 30 years, however, an immense landfill project transformed it into the city's fashionable district, thus providing much needed living space for the then overpopulated city. Soon, indeed, the well-to-do moved there from Beacon Hill and the South End.

In contrast to the tangled maze of lanes of the "old" city, Back Bay, as it was still called, was meticulously planned in regimented lines inspired by the boulevards of Paris. Its residential area north of Boylston Street now offers perhaps the best display of Victorian architecture in the country.

Live and Sculpted Waterfowl

The **Public Garden** is far prettier than neighbouring Boston Common (see page 20). Still supported entirely by private donations, the country's original botanical garden boasts a wonderful selection of ornamental flowerbeds, rare trees, and lush lawns. Weeping willows hang over the lagoon, around which, in summer, you can make a soporific little tour on a Swan Boat, pedalled by a strapping young man or woman sitting within a fashioned swan at the rear. In winter, the swans are replaced by hardy skaters.

The garden's quirky sculptures and little fountains merit exploration. The most recent (and popular) is the cute bronze Mrs. Mallard accompanied by her eight ducklings (near the Charles and Beacon Street entrance), a tribute to Robert McCloskey's *Make Way for Ducklings*, a famous children's tale (on sale in all local bookshops) which relates the traumas of rearing a family of ducklings in Boston. Before you move on, how about tea at the Ritz? The city's most famous hotel overlooks the garden.

Churches and Skyscrapers

From the Public Garden, Boylston Street leads into the commercial and business part of Back Bay. Follow it a short way to **Copley Square**, a popular summer focal point for concerts, and a place where kids splash in the fountain. A feast of contrasting buildings competes for your attention.

There is one building you will have seen already. Sleek, blue **John Hancock Tower**, New England's tallest building, acts as a striking beacon on many of the city's skyscapes. Two sides are knife-edge thin, and from certain vantage points it seems as if the building does a virtual disappearing act. When it was built in 1976 the blue glass had a tendency to fall out, so every sheet had to be replaced. If the weather is fine, pay a visit to the **Observatory** on the 60th floor. There's no better way to get to grips with Boston's peculiar topography. A model of the city in 1775 brings home just how much of the present land was at one time water.

There used to be fears that the tower would eclipse its neighbour, but the stature of **Trinity Church**, now reflected in the tower's glass, has only been enhanced. The church itself is grandiose. Designed in 1877 by Henry Hobson Richardson, America's leading architect of the day, it was quite in keeping with the aspirations of Back Bay at that time. Its style is taken from a number of French Romanesque churches, both in its ruddy brown exterior and interior, the decoration of which was masterminded by John La Farge, with frescoes and a marvellous ensemble of stained glass.

Another building worth visiting is the **Boston Public Library** (BPL; the oldest free municipal library in the world) facing the church on the other side of the square. Italian Renaissance in style and built on a bombastic scale, it houses a double marble staircase which climbs to a huge barrel-vaulted reading room and, on the third floor, a mural series by John Singer Sargent.

Copley Place, on Huntington Avenue, is equally monumental. It is made up of two 1,000-room hotels, a hundred shops, and acres of residential and office space. It's connected to the graceless **Prudential Center** by an overhead walkway. (The Pru was originally designed by architect I. M. Pei.) After touring the shops, go up to the Top of The Hub bar and restaurant and **Skywalk** (open Monday–Saturday, 10:00 A.M.–10:00 P.M., Sunday, noon–10:00 P.M.). As well as being

Despite the size of the John Hancock Tower, Boston's present will never overshadow its past.

a great vantage point from which to see the Hancock Tower, the Skywalk is more peaceful and spacious than the neighbouring observatory, though the views are less impressive.

A little further along Huntington Avenue, the **Christian Science World Headquarters** may not sound enticing (and indeed, the austerity of the administration buildings around a vast reflecting pool makes a sombre first impression), but the huge basilica of the Mother Church and the dwarfed Romanesque church—the original Mother Church—stand in sharp contrast. The former can hold 5,000; its tiered seating makes it more like a theatre than a place of worship.

Other than quotations on the walls from the New Testament and Christian Science founder, Mary Baker Eddy, there are no decorations. Some can be seen in the stained glass of the older church, the holy of holies, but these were discarded as the faith grew. Here, too, is Mary Baker Eddy's chair; she only ever addressed a congregation twice, as she tried to avoid personal idolatry. A guided tour is highly recommended (you can only visit the original church by joining a tour).

The Christian Science publishing building, to the right as you exit the church, holds the oddest of things: a glass

Window dressing along Newbury Street is as much of an art as choosing names.

globe, 9 meters (30 feet) in diameter, that you can walk through on a bridge. The **Mapparium** illustrates a multi-coloured world in which borders are drawn as they were in 1935. Glass doesn't absorb sound, so the acoustics are fun.

The Chic and the Victorian

A stroll along the length of **Newbury Street**—the city's most expensive real estate—is the most civilized and congenial of Boston experiences. This is where the chic and the conservative come to furnish their homes with art and antiques, wrap their bodies in designer fashion, have their hair styled in upmarket salons, and wine, dine, and drink iced coffee al fresco in summer. An obsession with image and appearance is redolent in both the tiny showcase shop windows and the people looking at them. Every display—whether for fine art, ice-cream, or tailoring—is worth a picture. Some of the galleries exhibit works by major artists. Notice the architecture as well: at the end of the converted carriage houses, the less genteel eastern end gives way to series of alternate classic bow- and flat-fronted townhouses.

Take a detour along the way down one of the side streets, alphabetically arranged from A to H, starting at the Public Garden (they're named after English peers). In between the avenues, look out for the narrow, arrow-straight service alleys that form the entranceway to the old servants' quarters at the backs of the houses. The strip which is lined with elms and runs down the spine of **Commonwealth Avenue** is the perfect vantage point on which to stand back and gaze at the various fancy Victorian buildings built in French Second Empire and Gothic styles. You can get a wonderful feel for what a Victorian Back Bay home was like in the fully furnished rooms of the **Gibson House**, at 137 Beacon Street, not far from the Public Garden (open for tours May–Octo-

LEADING MUSEUMS AND GALLERIES

Children's Museum, *300 Congress Street, Waterfront.* MBTA: South Station. Fun and didactic "hands-on" museum. Daily 10am-5pm (Fri 9pm); closed Mon July-Aug. Adults $7; 2-15/seniors $6; under 2, $2. (See page 45)

Computer Museum, *Museum Wharf, 300 Congress Street.* MBTA: South Station. Exhibits include a walk-through computer, robots, and games. Tues-Sun, 10am-5pm adults $7; children/seniors $5; under 5 free; Sun 3pm-5pm admission half price. (See page 45)

Harvard University Art Museums. MBTA: Harvard Square (Red Line). Fogg Art Museum: European/North American art; Busch-Reisinger: German art; Arthur M. Sackler: Classical, Asian and Islamic art. Mon-Sat 10am-5pm; Sun 1pm-5pm Entry $5 adults over 18; $4 seniors, $3 students $2.50; free before noon Sat. (See page 63)

Harvard University Museums of Natural History, *entrances at 24 Oxford Street* and at *11 Divinity Ave., Cambridge.* MBTA: Harvard Square. Four collections: see the American Indian display, glass plants, and prehistoric bones. Mon-Sat 9am-4:30pm, Sun 1pm-4:30pm; adults $5; students/seniors $3; children $1. (See page 64)

Isabella Stewart Gardner Museum, *280 The Fenway.* MBTA: Museum. A collection of masterpieces idiosyncratically displayed in a beautiful mansion. Tues-Sun 11am-5pm; adults $7; students/seniors $5; 12-17 years $3; under 12 free. (See page 56)

Museum of Fine Arts, *465 Huntington Ave.* MBTA: Museum. Comprehensive art and sculpture collections, Boston's finest; superb Asian and Egyptian galleries, and rooms full of Impressionist works. Closed Mon; open Tues-Sun 10am-4:45pm, (Wed 9:45pm); tours 10am-4pm; adults $8; seniors $6; 6-17 $3.50; pay as you wish Wed 4pm-9:45pm (See page 55)

Museum of Science, *Science Park, across Charles River.* MBTA: Science Park. This vast complex is a paean to the world of science. Daily 9am-5pm (Fri 9pm); adults $8;seniors $6; children 14 and under free. Planetarium and Omni Theatre: adults $7.50; seniors/children 14 and under$5.50. (See page 67)

New England Aquarium, *Central Wharf.* MBTA: Aquarium. Global underwater habitats; dolphin and sea lion presentations.9am-5pm Mon-Fri (Thur 8pm), 9am-6pm weekends and holidays. Adults $8.50; 3-11 $4.50. (See page 43) ber, Wednesday–Sunday at 1:00, 2:00, and 3:00 P.M., weekends the rest of the year). The contents of the house are the fascinating and colourful legacy of three generations of Gibsons, who lived here from 1860 to 1954.

AROUND BACK BAY

Fenway

Come to Fenway to enjoy the city's two superb and utterly distinct art museums, located by the thin, meandering tract of ponds, reeds, and meadows of the Back Bay Fens, and to see the Red Sox in action at Fenway Park. Its centre, Kenmore Square, pinpointed from afar by a massive neon CITGO sign, is a traffic-ridden, run-down intersection of fast-food parlours, frequented by punks and university students.

The **Museum of Fine Arts** (or MFA) contains one of the most important art collections in the country. There's much—too much—to absorb in one visit, so choose particular galleries or take a Highlights Tour leaflet and pick out just a few works. For example, the museum's outstanding collections of Asian works include Japanese armour, Javanese statue gods, Thai buddhas, and Indian elephants. Amongst the early North African items are first-rate Egyptian galleries with mummies and early sculpture, and Nubian statues and stelae.

Closer to home, you can see a cupboard of silverware fashioned by Paul Revere, and a famous portrait of the silversmith (among many others) by John Singleton Copley, probably Boston's best-known artist. The complete pantheon of European art is represented—from the Italian Renaissance to English landscape painters—but the most overwhelming rooms are those which exhibit works by 19th-century French artists, with dozens of Monets, Millet's *The Sower*, Renoir's *Dance at Bougival,* and works by

Cézanne, Toulouse-Lautrec, and Van Gogh. There's also a great museum shop, a café, and a restaurant.

Nowhere else in Boston can match the beauty of the courtyard in the **Isabella Stewart Gardner Museum**. Modelled on a Venetian loggia, the cloister, delicate arches, and salmon pink walls enclose a stunning, atmospheric space filled with foliage and classical statuary. Isabella Gardner created Fenway Court in 1903 to hold her outstanding collection of art. A flamboyant New Yorker, her unconventional ways scandalized the Bostonian brahmin set on more than one occasion. Her portrait by John Singer Sargent (in the Gothic Room) captures her individuality and her eccentricity lives on in her will, which stipulates that all of the 2,000 pieces on display in the house must be left exactly where they are. This decree is qualified by the condition that were anything to change, the museum's contents would be sold off, with the proceeds going to Harvard University. It's a most strange place to find a treasure-trove of world-famous artists' works: it feels something like a fusty, poorly lit English country house, and the labelling is cursory. Each

No matter where you are—downtown or the suburbs—you can find a peaceful spot to rest.

of the rooms has a particular theme or style—Dutch, Gothic, Early Italian, and so forth. The very names of some, such as the Titian, Raphael, or Veronese rooms, manage to convey the quality of the art work that they contain.

A Night Out with the Red Sox

Leave the car behind and experience being crushed by fans in a trolley on the MBTA Green Line to Kenmore. Constructed in 1912, Fenway Park is the oldest ballpark in the country. The quirky, irregularly shaped arena boasts real, manicured grass and a towering wall that is nicknamed the Green Monster for its scale and colour. This is an intimate place, so even those who are standing at the back will be close to the action. If you're not familiar with baseball's finer points, most fans in the friendly, vociferous, 34,000-strong crowd would love to talk you through them. In a low-scoring game dominated by the pitchers, you might wonder what the fuss is about. Feel the fever generated by a slick double-play or a home-run, and you could be hooked. For tickets, see page 123.

Bay Village and the South End

This is a chance to get right off the beaten tourist track for an exploration of the largely unheralded charms of a couple of residential neighbourhoods.

The few blocks of tiny **Bay Village** lie well hidden in between the Theater District and Back Bay, around Winchester, Melrose, and Fayette streets. It feels somewhat like a toy village—a miniature, flat version of Beacon Hill—with similar red-brick and black-shuttered homes lining pavements that are adorned with trees and old-fashioned street lamps. However, these were the homes of artisans, not brahmins, and are less precious, devoid of fancy wrought iron and cornicing. When the marsh of Back Bay was filled in during the 1860s, water flooded into this area, forcing the streets and houses to be raised on pilings.

Pursue Tremont Street south and cross over the Massachusetts Turnpike and you're in the **South End**. Come if for no other reason than simply to savour one (or more) of its great restaurants—a clutch of chic bistros on Tremont Street (at Clarendon Street). Those with a more adventurous palate will want to explore a number of ethnic establishments serving Korean, Ethiopian, and Syrian cuisine.

Like so much of Boston, in the middle of the 19th century the South End began as a landfill project, but it soon lost out in desirability to Back Bay. Its present population is a multi-ethnic mix of Hispanic, Irish, West Indian, and Greek, as well as Boston's largest gay community. Some districts—to the south of Shawmut Avenue, for example—are best avoided. In others, though, you will come across bright community murals and perhaps a reggae band playing in a local park.

The neighbourhood in general boasts (justifiably) America's greatest concentration of Victorian terraces. Bow brick houses, their steep stoops (or steps) framed with scrolled black railings, are surrounded by stretches of green park, the finest examples being Union Park Square, situated just off Tremont Street, and both Rutland and Concord squares farther to the south.

THE CLOSE-IN SUBURBS

Although the Boston suburbs might not claim any "must see" sights, if you have a car and are confident about managing to find your way around with a good map, there are a variety of intriguing places to explore.

South Boston, referred to as Southie, is in fact (rather confusingly) situated east of Downtown. Home to the likes of establishments such as Flanagan's Supermarket and the Shannon Tavern on its main thoroughfare of East Broadway, it is not difficult to guess what nationality has set down its roots here. Follow the high street past its old wooden and brick houses and down to **Fort Independence**, standing at the very mouth of Boston Inner Harbor. The fort is rarely open, but join the locals who settle down in the surrounding park with deck chairs and binoculars to watch the mesmerizing, endless nautical and aeronautic activity.

Your next stop could well be **Dorchester Heights**, a three-tiered tower of marble (fenced off) standing on a hill. It was from here in 1776 that George Washington was successful in his plight to frighten British troops into evacuating Boston by placing artillery trained on the city (see page 17).

If you follow the waterfront south, you will find yourself at the extraordinary, stark white building that houses the **John F. Kennedy Library and Museum** (open 9:00 A.M.–5:00 P.M.). Positioned right on the edge of the bay, the light and colours of the sea flood its atrium. This eulogistic museum, which was recently redesigned to appeal to a younger generation that wasn't around when Kennedy was alive, re-creates his Oval Office and shows lots of video footage of the man in action (see page 115 for details of boat trips from Downtown).

Situated not far away to the west is Franklin Park, parts of which are considered unsafe, though you won't need to worry if you stick to the **Zoo** (open daily, 10:00 A.M.–4:00 P.M.; 10:00–5:00 P.M., Saturday, Sunday, and holidays). Although it's more park than zoo, the showpiece is a splendid African tropical rainforest, which is complete with gorillas and warthogs, and nearby lies a giant walk-through bird cage. Franklin Park was supposed to be the jewel in the **Emerald Necklace**, the last in a 11-km (7-mile) network of parks by Frederick Law Olmsted that run all the way from Boston Common.

Olmsted has actually been called the father of landscape architecture. During the 19th century he was instrumental in the shaping of many American cities: his best known creation (with Calvert Vaux) was New York's Central Park. He would have admired the flourishing 107 hectares (265 acres) of **Arnold Arboretum**, west of Franklin Park. Each of the 15,000 trees, shrubs, and vines, divided into individual clusters, is scientifically documented.

Before returning to Boston, make a final stop in affluent Brookline (actually a separate town), once home to Olmsted. The modest wooden house at 83 Beals Street (property of the National Park Service, open 10:00 A.M.–4:30 P.M., mid-May–October) is the **John F. Kennedy National Historic Site**. This is his birthplace and where he lived until the age of four. His mother, Rose, had it restored, partly with furniture which was used by the family at the time.

CAMBRIDGE

Although it's only separated from Boston by a river and a few subway stops, Cambridge is a separate city with a separate outlook, fashioned by the presence of two of America's most respected academic establishments. Its network of distinct communities is worth exploring, but by far the most alluring is Harvard Square.

Harvard Square

What makes rather unkempt Harvard Square special is the people. This is a place where everyone just hangs out, from students conversing in sententious tones, to punks in leather, and professionals in pristine suits. Street performers—fire jugglers, puppeteers, trapeze artists, musicians (Joni Mitchell and Tracy Chapman both once played here)—pull big crowds, notably on weekend evenings.

There are innumerable cafés and bookshops (see page 87) in which to whittle away several hours. Buy a newspaper from the global selection in Out of Town News in the centre of the actual Harvard Square (the name also refers to all the surrounding streets), and settle down at Au Bon Pain café. It's *the* place for people-watching, and for a couple of dollars you can also pit your wits against the resident chess maestro.

Harvard University

Superlatives are exhausted by an attempt to describe Harvard University. Of all the country's academic establishments, it is the oldest (founded in 1636 as a training ground for puritan ministers) the richest (with a huge $5 billion in endowments) and it can also lay claim to the most Nobel Prize winners. Like most colleges in the United States, the university offers scholarships, but these are limited to a lucky few.

Harvard Yard

The oldest part of the university backs on to Harvard Square. When the weather's fine, students lounge decorously on the

Cambridge is a cerebral place – shown here is an impromptu chess match in Harvard Square.

Stately Memorial Church is one of many historic buildings at Harvard.

courtyard grass in bright sunlight dappled by mature trees, or ostentatiously read leaning against building pillars. Visitors can wander freely, or be taken on a guided tour (see page 114).

Most of the red brick buildings in the Old Yard house students. Look out for the statue in front of the grey University Hall. According to the inscription on the plaque, it's "John Harvard, founder, 1638." In fact, it isn't John Harvard, but a student who posed for the sculptor, and since Harvard himself wasn't the founder but the first benefactor, and the date is wrong anyway, it has been nicknamed "The Statue of Three Lies" (all this in spite of Harvard's motto: *Veritas*, the Latin for "Truth").

The adjacent New Yard is possibly even more beautiful. Here, the colossal pillars of the **Widener Library** (Monday–Friday, 9:00 A.M.–10:00 P.M.; Saturday, 9:00 A.M.–5:00 P.M.; Sunday, noon–5:00 P.M.) gaze over the grass towards the Memorial Church, above which an elegant white spire reaches up out of the foliage. Widener is the largest university library in the world. It's named after Harry Widener, who drowned with the sinking of the *Titanic*. His mother subseqently funded the establishment of the library, with the proviso that no Harvard student would be allowed to graduate without learning to swim. You can inspect Harry's book collection in a peaceful panelled room. Amongst its many works are a 1623 Shakespeare folio and a Gutenberg Bible of 1450.

Art and Science

One ticket allows you to see all of Harvard's art treasures. The most enjoyable museum is the **Fogg** on Quincy Street, just off the northeast corner of Harvard Yard. It runs the gamut of European and North American art from medieval to modern times, but is composed well enough to be digestible in one visit. You can expect well-known works: Rembrandt and Dürer prints, Rodin sculptures, and pieces by Picasso, Matisse, Chagall, and Léger in the modern section. In the decorative arts, keep an eye open for the President's Chair, a medieval contraption embellished with various knobs and rings on which the incumbent Harvard president has to sit each year for ceremonies.

Through at the back of the Fogg lies the **Busch-Reisinger Museum**, dealing with the modern art of northern and central Europe. It is especially noted for Expressionist works by Klimt, Kandinsky, and Klee.

James Stirling, the famous British post-modern architect, created a building that is at once bold and sensitive to its old neighbours for the nearby **Arthur M. Sackler Museum**. It holds a compact but important collection of classical and ancient works of art of Asian and Islamic origin, the ancient Chinese artifacts like neolithic jades and earthenware vessels being particularly rewarding.

Just outside the Sackler is **Memorial Hall**, a monument of cathedral-like proportions set under a multi-coloured roof and built to commemorate former students who died on the

Union side in the Civil War. If it's open, peek inside at the lovely wooden Sanders Theater and the vast reception hall.

A few steps north up Oxford Street or Divinity Avenue, the four **Harvard University Museums of Natural History** are conveniently grouped together under one roof. Each merits a visit on its own; reserve a good few hours to do them justice. The best part of the Archeology and Ethnology Museum is the Hall of North American Indians, with its beautiful totem poles, cradles and dolls, and explanations of the differences between the lifestyles of the various tribes.

Don't miss the meteorites in the Mineral and Geological Museums. In addition, the Botanical Museum harbours a world-renowned collection of glass replicas of plants and fruits, as well as delicate flowers, moulded and coloured to baffling perfection. The 3,000 pieces were made as teaching aids but are works of art in their own right. Children like the prehistoric fossil bones, the whale skeletons, and the menagerie of stuffed beasts in the Zoology Museum.

In and Around Brattle Street

The Brattle Theater, standing at the Harvard Square end of Brattle Street, was formerly a playhouse. It now shows old films, one of which inspired the Casablanca bar/restaurant and its fun murals. Another lovely wooden building a little further up is the Blacksmith House Bakery, the home of the blacksmith on whom Longfellow based "Under the spreading chestnut tree the village smithy stands"—although the tree is long gone. Brattle Street soon becomes more residential. Of the fine mansions along the way, a few were occupied by loyalists at the time of the Revolution, which is why the street was dubbed Tory Row.

One such residence is the yellow clapboard **Longfellow House**, which was commandeered by Washington as his

Longfellow House—home of the venerable American poet and temporary headquarters for George Washington.

headquarters during the siege of Boston (see page 16). Known for being home for 45 years to Henry Wadsworth Longfellow, one of America's best-loved poets, the house still has many of his original belongings: furniture, books, carpets, and even the wallpaper. Incidentally, the chair in his study was made with wood from the chestnut tree of *The Village Blacksmith* poem. Summer concerts and poetry readings are organized in the pretty garden.

Take the car or a bus west down Brattle Street to Victorian **Mount Auburn Cemetery**, a "garden cemetery" which is one of the most beautiful burial places imaginable. At the entrance, pick up a horticultural map that will help to guide you around the acres of landscaped banks, ponds, and superb trees. At the same time, get a map locating the graves of famous people, including Longfellow, Mary Baker Eddy, and Isabella Gardner.

Heading back down Brattle Street: on the left is **Radcliffe Yard**, an elegant octagon of buildings carefully set around watered lawns. Radcliffe was established back in

1879 as a women-only college; now it has become affiliated to Harvard, though graduates receive degrees from both places. Exit from Radcliffe Yard out on to **Cambridge Common**, where Washington first inspected the troops on 3 July 1775 (the elm tree that supposedly marks the site is not the original). Following Garden Street east you will come to Anglican Christ Church, which during the Revolution was turned into a barracks by the colonists. Next door the burial ground is referred to as God's Acre; it is the resting place of early Harvard presidents and Revolutionary soldiers.

If you've time to spare, get a feel for the best of urban America in the network of lovely side streets off Massachusetts Avenue to the north, studded with glorious, ancient wooden houses. If you're looking for an evening alternative to Harvard Square, try checking out the various ethnic restaurants scattered around here, as well as the interesting, fun Hispanic flavour of **Inman Square**, located down Cambridge Street.

East Cambridge

The stretch of Cambridge that lies on the Charles River lacks the charm of Harvard Square but has some interesting buildings and good museums.

The **Massachusetts Institute of Technology** (M.I.T.) is America's leading science and engineering establishment. Its campus feels markedly different from Harvard, with modern architecture and numbered buildings (M.I.T. settled here in 1916). Maps for self-guided tours are available from the Information Center (located in the Rogers Building, 77 Massachusetts Avenue). Off campus is the small M.I.T. Museum (265 Massachusetts Avenue, open Tuesday–Friday, 10:00 A.M.–5:00 P.M., noon–5:00 P.M.), with exciting scientific displays. To the west of the Rogers Building, the striking, glass-sided Kresge Auditorium and circular, moated brick chapel are worth a look.

A Henry Moore sculpture rests in Killian Court, east of the Rogers Building. Some of the more outlandish architecture was designed by former student I. M. Pei (such as the Weisner Building, where contemporary art exhibitions are held). Pei was also responsible for famous projects such as the glass pyramid at the Louvre in Paris and Boston's own controversial Government Center.

A shuttle bus runs between Kendall Square, at the eastern edge of the M.I.T. campus, and the CambridgeSide Galleria. The impressive waterside mall, which features a number of large department stores and many smaller specialty shops, is the former site of the **New England Sports Museum,** which has relocated across the river to FleetCenter (see page 91), the new home of Boston sports franchises the Celtics, of the National Basketball Association, and the Bruins of the National Hockey League..

You could spend the best part of a day in the **Museum of Science** complex that spans the Charles River. Of the 400-plus exhibits, some—such as those on mathematics and biotechnology—would stimulate an M.I.T. graduate, while many others appeal to young children. The museum advocates and pioneers hands-on learning. Highlights include: superb 250,000 times life-size insect models; a variety of dinosaur models and fossils; exercises in the Human Body Room which demonstrate how various parts of the body function; stimulating games for learning about energy; a rainforest re-creation. The world's biggest Van de Graaff generator reaches up through three floors in the Theater of Electricity: Try to be there at the right time for a lightning show.

There are also laser shows and star-gazing in the Planetarium, while the Mugar Omni Theater will whisk you off to beautiful new worlds through a huge, all-enveloping screen. Gentle river trips with good views of Back Bay leave from the galleria and the Science Museum (see page 115).

EXPLORING MASSACHUSETTS

If you only make one trip from Boston, then make sure it's to the two little towns of Lexington and Concord. The towns' landmarks, which commemorate the skirmishes of 19 April 1775 (the day the War of American Independence began), are a natural extension of the Freedom Trail and stand with the nation's most significant.

The best way to get here and around—the sites are spread out—is by car (half an hour from Boston on Route 2 and Route 4/225). You can see the main historical sights in a day, but you'll need a second visit to appreciate Concord's rich literary heritage. During the summer and every year on Patriot's Day (see page 89), colourful staged battles and military encampments are arranged, in which the militiamen practise their drill. Telephone (508) 369-3120 for further details.

The coast, meanwhile, has much to offer and makes for some great excursions.

Lexington

First port of call on route from Boston is the **Museum of Our National Heritage**. The "Let it Begin Here" exhibit provides the historical background to the day's sightseeing.

In the early days, the first sign of resistance came at **Lexington Battle Green**. Captain Parker lined up 77 Minutemen (ready "at a minute's notice") against the 700 English soldiers. His orders were: "Stand your ground! Don't fire unless fired upon! But if they mean to have a war, let it

The Tap Room at the Buckman Tavern looks much as it would have in 1775.

begin here." A shot was fired and eight colonials subsequently died.

The triangular green, surrounded by lovely white timber houses and with a steeple poking over verdant trees, is soaked with patriotic images. Under a Stars and Stripes banner flying on a lofty pole, a plaque simply says "Birthplace of American liberty." A burial monument honours "The first victims to the sword of British tyranny and oppression," and a defiant Minuteman keeps a look-out down the main street in the direction from which the Redcoats appeared. You can join guided tours around three lovely wooden buildings, all furnished with period pieces, that played a role on the fateful day: these are the **Buckman Tavern**, where the Minutemen gathered prior to the English arrival; the **Munroe Tavern**, where some Redcoats recuperated on their way back from Concord; and the **Hancock-Clark House**, in which John Hancock and Samuel Adams were sleeping when Paul Revere arrived. Oxen were used to move the house in 1896 because it spoiled a neighbour's view; it was brought back to its original spot in 1974.

Concord

Battle Road, much of it following Route 2A, joins Lexington to Concord, part of the Minuteman National Historic Park. Along the road, on the afternoon of 19 April 1775, patriot troops harried the retreating English. To get your bearings, visit the Battle Road Visitor Center. On the way to Concord, you could stop off at the Paul Revere Capture site and Hartwell Tavern, a typical, unpainted, period country inn.

On your arrival in Concord, head for **Old North Bridge**, the other half of the national park. English troops, dispatched to search a farm for a store of arms, came up against Colonials at the bridge. After brief volleys of fire and a few casualties on each side, the English retreated.

This was where the Americans first resisted with force, firing "the shot heard 'round the world," as Ralph Waldo Emerson put it in his *Concord Hymn*. It's a peaceful, scenic spot, with a meandering river amidst meadows covered in purple loosestrife. Go across the rickety bridge (not the original) to look at the Minuteman Statue, which is symbolically kitted out with rifle and plough (Emerson views them, a little romantically, as "embattled farmers"). Follow the path up to the Visitor Center in the mansion at the top of the hill, where you can watch a video about the battle and buy a Bill of Rights souvenir.

Literary Houses

Concord's literary heritage has proven notably longer-lasting than its military renown. Four lovely old houses, all of them furnished with period contents and original treasure-troves,

Turn back the clock at Old Sturbridge Village. You may never want to leave.

offer detailed, lengthy guided tours. Unless you've brushed up on 19th-century American authors, be selective.

The most beautifully sited is the **Old Manse**, in a field that is next door to North Bridge. Reverend William Emerson, who built it, watched the battle from the window; his grandson Ralph later lived here. The other three houses are situated close together on the outskirts of town, on or near to Route 2A going to Lexington. They are: **Emerson House**, quite a grand affair, which is full of Ralph's books and belongings; the enchanting, homely **Orchard House**, owned by the Alcotts (amongst them Louisa, who wrote *Little Women* here); and the **Wayside**, spanning around 170 years and once the property of not only the Alcotts, but also Nathaniel Hawthorne.

Concord town provides a charming antidote to an overdose of culture, with plenty of shops to browse through. Pack a picnic and follow Walden Street and then Route 126 to **Walden Pond**, a glorious lake fringed by little

The Mayflower II: not the real thing, but a close approximation.

sandy beaches and enclosed by thick woods (be warned: it can get very crowded). Here, Henry David Thoreau, philosopher, essayist, poet, and friend of Emerson, lived from 1845 to 1847, immersing himself in nature as described in his classic work, *Walden*. Near the main parking lot is a replica of his hut, containing a bed, table, desk, three chairs, and a stove.

Old Sturbridge Village

This is the closest Massachusetts comes to having a theme park. New England buildings along with painstaking reconstructions have created a beautiful village typical of the early 19th century. All the shops vital to a community are here, including a beamed tavern, a brick bank, a law office, a tinner's, and a cobbler's. In addition, dirt tracks lead up to a cooper's, a potter's, mills, a blacksmith's, and a farm. Animals graze and crops grow in the pastoral idyll. Everything feels as if its from the period except for the café's frozen yoghurt, and French fries.

"Locals" go about their business in the stores, homes, and cottage industries: blacksmiths firing horseshoes, the coopers making barrels. Watching and quizzing them on their tasks is a great way to understand how people once lived. The village lies on Route 20, roughly 1½ hours west of Boston. The admission fee may seem expensive, but don't forget that it is all in and covers everything. Allow yourself a full day here. For further information, telephone (800) SEE-1830 or (508) 347-3362, or visit the Sturbridge Village Web site at http://www.osv.org.

Plymouth

The city doesn't let you forget its famous heritage, for this is where the pilgrims arrived on the *Mayflower* and settled in 1620 to avoid religious persecution in England. Well positioned under an hour from Boston, both the first-rate museums and cheery gift shops that sell black, rimmed pilgrim hats and Mayflower ships in a bottle offer a satisfying, full day's sightseeing.

Start at **Mayflower II**, built in England, which was sailed across the Atlantic in 1957. The full-scale approximation of the original vessel gives a very good impression of the cramped conditions that the original 102 passengers had to endure on their 66-day journey. Wander the decks and talk to actors who play the parts of sailors and pilgrims. Nearby lies the enshrined **Plymouth Rock**—nothing much to look at, but since it's supposedly the first piece of land on which the pilgrims stepped in Plymouth, a worthy national symbol of civil and religious freedom.

"Welcome to the 17th century," announces a placard at **Plimoth Plantation**, a couple of miles south of town. For the villagers who are in the stockade of wattle and daub huts, it's still 1627. The plantations's characters chatter away about their religious beliefs and lifestyles as they tend their cows, sheep, and pigs in the nearby allotments. You can also meet Hobbamock, an Indian neighbour, in his campsite. The entrance fee is expensive, but the re-creation is superbly done and thoroughly worth it. Note that you can buy a joint ticket which covers both the plantation and *Mayflower II*.

Of the museums back in town, the **Pilgrim Hall Museum** is arguably the most important. There, you will find various pilgrims' possessions such as bibles and a cradle, and documents of original compacts from King James I to settlers. If you're looking for more diversions, there's also a busy harbour from where you can go whale watching, a waterside promenade, and inexpensive seafood restaurants.

Visit Plimoth Plantation and go back in time to see a settler busy with her daily chores.

Cape Cod

Fabulous beaches, invigorating breezes, sharp light, and the deliciously strong colours of canary-yellow sands, cobalt-blue seas, lime-green marshes; these are just a few of the reasons why the world

A sea of dunes around Race Point Light, seen from the Pilgrim Monument, Provincetown.

likes to come to Cape Cod. Thoreau summed it up as "The bare and bended arm of Massachusetts." Now, in summer, though, it is certainly not bare of people, who flock here for the lovely villages, art galleries, seafood, and rural lanes.

With good traffic—avoid the Friday evening mass exodus, especially in summer (see page 111)—it's only an hour from Boston to Sandwich, the nearest point on the Cape. With so many alluring inns, however, why not stop for a night or two? To appreciate the Cape's charms you need to indulge in a bit of "porch dwelling," see a ruby-red sunset, and get up for early morning mists. If you do intend to stay, be sure to book ahead in high season.

The best parts of the Cape are along the north shore and its "upper arm." Note some beach tips: The sheltered Cape Cod Bay beaches are transformed into mud flats when the tide is

Anything goes in Provincetown. The population here can increase 11-fold in the summer.

out; the spectacular east coast beaches can have a strong undertow; on a sunny summer's day parking lots for the east coast beaches can fill up entirely; on municipally run beaches, visitors usually have to buy a permit, which can be obtained from the town hall.

Turn on to **Route 6A** after the Sagamore Bridge. The villages along here roll into one another, a ribbon of pretty cottages, manicured lawns, and boutiques touting flowers, pottery, weathervanes—anything desirable. There are numerous side roads leading to beaches.

You're soon in **Sandwich**, the Cape's oldest community, with quaint, early vernacular buildings. A doll museum, a museum full of delicate glass products, and a collection of vintage cars, military artifacts, and local arts in the lovingly tended gardens of the Heritage Plantation are among the many and varied attractions.

Some of the handsome Victorian residences along **Brewster's** main street have been turned into upmarket country inns. At one time they were the homes of wealthy sea captains. Today this is the Cape's richest community.

Cut across the mainland to **Chatham**, at the start of the Outer or (confusingly) Lower Cape. This well-to-do town, edged on three sides by water, has a civilized main street and plenty of unadorned, weatherbeaten houses—the most simple in the traditional "saltbox" style. At Fish Pier, in a picturesque natural channel that is protected by a barrier beach, tourists in ringside seats on an observation deck watch the catch being unloaded. Chatham Light, to the south, also enjoys a view, over a popular beach. Boats ferry visitors to Monomoy Island from Morris Island to observe birdlife.

At the **Cape Cod National Seashore** you can listen to the Cape's classic sound of pounding waves breaking on awesome beaches that are backed by mountainous dunes. Due to the fragility of the dunes, access is strictly controlled, limited to boardwalks at certain points. The two Park Information Centers have maps which locate the beaches. Salt Pond, near Eastham, has a cramped but comprehensive exhibition showing both the natural and human features of the region. Not far from Provincetown, at Province Lands, take the opportunity to climb on to the roof for a panoramic view of the dunes, tenuously held together by pitch pines and oaks.

Not a bad vantage point—an eagle-eyed lifeguard on the Cape Cod National Seashore.

An even better view is offered if you climb the Pilgrim Monument in **Provincetown**. Although from a distance it is a mere matchstick, it becomes a 77 meter (253 foot) tower close up. From on top, you can see the sea in every direction and beneath, a little town cowering from the elements in the fold of a cupped hand. Though the pilgrims settled in Plymouth in favour of more fertile pastures, they landed here first. The museum at the base of the tower recounts the story.

P-Town, as it is sometimes called, is all things to all people. Families like it as a holiday resort, with stores selling T-shirts, and scrimshaw and driftwood curios, and there are fishing and whale-watch trips galore. That's only one view, though, for this is also a mecca of alternative culture, a place where you can have psychic readings done and buy astrology charts; where same-sex couples walk the streets hand in hand and outrageous transvestites drum up trade for cabaret shows. There are numerous art galleries, some of which have excellent work, notably those in the East End.

Singing Beach, one of the loveliest on the North Shore

In summer, this melting pot fills the town to the brim and every guest-house displays a "Sorry" sign in its window. In winter, there's room to breathe with just the residents for company—many of them artists and Portuguese fishermen and restauranteurs. You can come to Provincetown on a day trip from Boston (see page 114), but if you don't stay longer, you'll miss half the fun.

For a less frenetic pace, visit **Wellfleet**, a few miles south. It has its own share of galleries and beatniks, but is decidedly more lackadaisical, complete with an unpretentious fishing harbour in a scenic inlet.

North Shore

Past the ugly northern suburbs of Boston lies a lovely rocky coastline from Marblehead to Cape Ann, with picturesque ports, fine sandy beaches, and the elegant, sprawling homes of wealthy Bostonians.

Although commuter trains (see page 125) run from Boston to Salem, Manchester, Gloucester, and Rockport, in the majority of cases you are debouched a long way from beaches and sights. In summer, the traffic isn't quite as appalling as on Cape Cod, but that's not saying much.

From Boston, follow Route 1A then 129 to **Marblehead**. The first people to settle here were Cornish fishermen. Now you can hardly see the water for moored yachts; halyards clink and large cars are parked outside exclusive sailing clubs. The superb natural harbour is formed by Marblehead Neck, covered in a host of big residences and with a little park at its tip. The port's loveliest feature, though, is the Old Town, with its narrow, sloping streets and various pristine coloured houses dating from the early 18th century. Each one carries a wooden plaque depicting a fish, the date the house was built, and the names and occupations of the owners.

A Bewitching City

At **Salem**, magic bookshops, fortune tellers, a witch house, dungeon, and museum, even a costumed vampire all recall the towns infamous witchcraft trials of 1692. A red-painted **Heritage Trail** line runs between the main attractions, as in Boston's Freedom Trail, but many, though entertaining, do not have any historical basis. The trail also visits relics of the town's maritime tradition—it was once one of America's main ports. There's too much to absorb in one day, but follow it nonetheless to appreciate Salem's lovely old streets, and visit the following sights.

Start off from the National Park Visitors Center at Museum Place (on Essex Street), where you can collect background literature and a map of the Heritage Trail. First, visit the **Peabody** and **Essex Museums**, the former an extensive, superb synopsis of maritime Salem, the latter with original witchcraft documents. Kids always love the **Salem Witch Museum**, a first-rate diorama show with scenes from 1692.

Author Nathaniel Hawthorne.

Continue beyond the disappointing maritime sights to the **House of the Seven Gables**, which was made famous by Nathaniel Hawthorne's eponymous novel. The 17th-century house is now surrounded by other

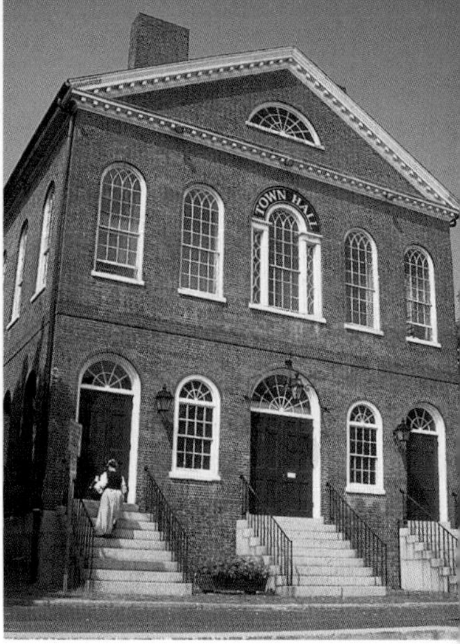

Salem Witch Museum (above); Salem Town Hall, (right) where "witchcraft trials" are held.

similarly aged buildings, including the home in which Hawthorne was born.

The trail brings you back to the lovely, red-brick market-place, where the trial of Bridget Bishop is re-enacted (with the audience judging her fate). Lastly, kids again will take to the **Witch Dungeon Museum**. After a show, a tour takes you through eerie, re-created cells where the guilty were imprisoned. Some are no bigger than a telephone booth.

Cape Ann

From Salem, the coast road to Cape Ann goes through Manchester, with the lovely, sandy Singing Beach. Just past Magnolia, stop off at **Hammond Castle Museum**, an ostentatious mix of Gothic church, Renaissance chateau, and medieval castle, built by inventor John Hays Hammond, Jr.

Gloucester is the country's oldest fishing port and also the busiest on the Massachusetts coast. Rows of gulls sit on the ridges of the factory roofs that line the wooden quays and jetties, while a steady stream of fishing craft and whale-watch cruisers come in and out. The big rustic cafés are fine places to eat chowder, oysters, clams, and crabs. In the Rocky Neck Art Colony on the south side of the harbour, painters wearing braces and straw hats pose behind their easels.

Head south to Eastern Point and **Beauport**. There, a guided tour takes you through most of 40 elaborate small rooms covering every conceivable architectural style. Built to impress and entertain, it was only ever lived in by one man.

Take the southern coast road to **Rockport** and you'll pass the sandy Good Harbor Beach and Long Beach. Rockport's harbour is as pretty as a picture, and Motif #1, a red shack covered with brightly coloured lobster floats, is one of New England's most painted images—hence its name.

A big catch, Rockport.

Visitors swamp the port in summer, particularly Bearskin Neck alongside the harbour. Miniature gabled and flower-decked huts line this very pretty tourist trap, each selling just one type of item—scrimshaw, fudge, leather, pewter, and especially art. When you've finished shopping, ask for The Paper House, a chalet and its contents entirely constructed from 100,000 newspapers.

WHAT TO DO

SHOPPING

When and Where to Shop

Most shops open between 9:00 A.M. and 10:00 A.M. and close between 5:30 P.M. and 7:00 P.M. On the whole, department stores remain open until 7:00 P.M. Some of the main malls, like Faneuil Hall Marketplace, stay open until 9:00 P.M. every night of the week, and from noon to 6:00 P.M. on Sundays.

The pedestrianized city centre around **Downtown Crossing**, along Washington, Winter, and Summer streets, has major chain department stores such as Filene's and Jordan Marsh—New England's largest—as well as a selection of lovely old-fashioned shops scattered down the sidestreets.

Faneuil Hall Marketplace is a great place to shop for gifts; its plethora of themed boutiques selling kites, boxer shorts, decorative pigs, hand-made Irish woollens, and a host of other arts and crafts items makes gift shopping much easier than it can be elsewhere.

In Back Bay, the rather soulless, marbled atrium of **Copley Place** holds over a hundred shops, a considerable number of which are ostentatious outlets for the mainstream fashion chains. The new arcades in the **Prudential Center** accompany the upmarket department stores of Lord and Taylor and Saks Fifth Avenue.

Shopping in the Back Bay area, however, is synonymous with strolling along **Newbury Street**. Here you can study the eye-catching window displays of the various art galleries, antique shops, and avant-garde, designer boutiques that line the roadside.

In Cambridge, the impressive atriumed **CambridgeSide Galleria** is the site of department stores and many clothes

Looking for a gift? You can't go wrong at the shopping carts and boutiques at Faneuil Hall.

shops. In the area of **Harvard Square** meanwhile, there are many student-oriented shops.

What to Buy

Art and Antiques: all along Newbury Street, a selection of priceless pieces of art suited to the pockets of professional collectors are hidden in attention-grabbing windows which are works of art in their own right. Here you will also find exceptional antiques.

It is to Charles Street on Beacon Hill that you should head for inexpensive bric-a-brac and old prints. The Museum of Fine Arts shop (also in Copley Place) offers reproduction sculptures, paintings and jewellery, as well as books.

Clothes: one of the most impressive and expensive clothes shops, in a grandiose building that was once the Museum of Natural History, is Louis Boston, at 234 Berkeley Street (off Newbury Street). If you're after something trendy—possibly a jacket from a Massachusetts designer or a dress by a European label—head for the boutiques on Newbury Street. For bargains, don't miss Filene's Basement (see page 37).

Jewellery: at the Jewelers Exchange, located at 333 Washington Street, you'll discover a mini-mall of retail shops. The swankiest jeweller's is Tiffany & Company in Copley Place.

Music: CDs are generally a better buy here in the U.S. than in Europe. Visit the enormous Tower Records, 360 Newbury Street (at Massachusetts Avenue), as well as the discount stores around Harvard Square.

Seafood: the restaurant chain Legal Sea Foods offers to ship live lobsters anywhere in the U.S. (tel. 254-7000/1-800-343-5804). Bay State Lobster, at 379-395 Commercial Street (tel. 523-7960), North End, provides the same service, and is worth a visit simply to see customers selecting their prey from giant tanks. You can, too.

Sports: souvenir shops selling paraphernalia like autographed photos and clothing from all of Boston's major league teams can be found at the arenas and in shopping centres.

Toys: a massive bear gives a wave at F.A.O. Schwarz, 440 Boylston Street, Back Bay, the city's best toy shop. Faneuil Hall Marketplace has toy boutiques in addition to a Disney store. The Science, Computer, and Children's museums all have great associated shops.

ENTERTAINMENT

For the latest information on what's happening where during your stay, consult Boston's leading papers and magazines for the range of entertainment listings (see page 116).

The Classical Repertoire

After New York, Boston offers the best **classical music** repertoire in the States. The Boston Symphony Orchestra (known as the B.S.O.) leads the way at Symphony Hall, one of the world's best acoustic venues. Serious pieces are performed in the winter season (including on Friday afternoons), while more popular performances—known as the **Boston Pops**—take place in May and June. At the beginning of July, the Pops moves to the Hatch Memorial Shell down at the riverside Esplanade; the performance for the Fourth of July draws many thousands of listeners. Both the Berklee College of Music and the New England Conservatory of Music put on outstanding performances. For a host of chamber and choral recitals across the city, consult up-to-date listings (see page 116). Two of the loveliest places to hear music are the Museum of Fine Arts, where period instruments are often used, and the Isabella Gardner Museum.

On of the prettiest of the many antiques shops on Charles Street, Beacon Hill.

Of the city's three principal **opera** companies, the Opera Company of Boston is said to have the best reputation. For **dance**, the Boston Ballet performs classical and modern pieces, and the Dance Umbrella group is renowned for the high quality of its innovative work.

Theatre

Bostonians have been known to complain that they only get raw shows on a trial run, pre-Broadway, or something that's already been round the world twice. In fact, the Colonial revival theatres dating from around 1900 near Tremont Street have had most of the famous actors and actresses from this century tread their boards.

Just as rewarding as the latest big musical in town are the works by professional resident companies such as the Huntington Theatre Company or the American Repertory Theatre at Harvard's Loeb Drama Center. *Shear Madness*

A Bibliophile's Paradise

Cambridge has more bookshops (24 at the last count) per capita than anywhere else in the U.S. (Its greatest competition probably comes from Boston.) Many specialize in topics—mystery, poetry, feminism, foreign literature, the occult—and most play a fundamental role in day-to-day life, acting not just as bookshops, but also as places to hang out and socialize. Many also stay open until 11pm seven nights a week.

BRATTLE BOOK SHOP, 9 West St., Downtown—an atmospheric treasure trove of antiquarian books.

B.U. BOOKSTORE, 660 Beacon St., Kenmore Square—Boston University's bookstore, the largest in New England, which also has a nice café.

GLOBE CORNER BOOKSTORE, 1 School St., Downtown—based in an historic building (see page 31) and specializing in literature on Boston and New England.

GROLIER POETRY BOOKSHOP, 6 Plympton St., Harvard Square—a tiny, atmospheric haunt of overflowing shelves.

WATERSTONE'S, 26 Exeter St. (at Newbury Street), Back Bay—a British shop; civilized and spacious.

WORDSWORTH BOOKS, 30 Brattle St., Harvard Square—stocks lots of discounted titles, good for bargain buys.

at the Charles Playhouse—a whodunnit set in a Newbury Street hair salon where the audience questions the suspects—is the longest-running non-musical show in American history.

Comedy

Some of the country's funniest performers appear in the best-known of the city's many comedy clubs, like Catch A Rising Star at the Charles Playhouse and the Comedy Connection at Faneuil Hall Marketplace. Try to find out in advance whether well-established professionals or local acts are performing. (The latter are often just as entertaining thanks to their insight into city mores.)

The Late-Night Scene

Cambridge has several great **jazz clubs**, such as the upmarket Regattabar in the Charles Hotel. Telephone the jazz hotline on 787-9700 for details.

For a more raucous time, try the gamut of clubs in **Boylston Place**, off Boylston Street on the edge of Boston Common. If you need a dose of high-energy dancing with a young set, the cavernous clubs in the Entertainment Zone on **Lansdowne Road**, alongside Fenway Park ballpark, are for you. Avalon (tel. 262-2424) is one of the largest and most popular night clubs, and has live music.

Thursday night is one of the liveliest in **bars**, as many people go away for the weekend. Arguably two of the most civilized haunts are the peaceful Ritz Bar, with its famous martini selection, and the Four Seasons Hotel piano bar. Both look on to the Public Garden.

You can rub shoulders with the politicians in The Last Hurrah over at the Omni Parker House (see page 131). If you like to mix with the fashionable set, try Biba (see page 141).

CALENDAR OF EVENTS

The Greater Boston Convention and Visitors Bureau publishes biannual travel planners which give the exact dates of all of the city's events and festivals throughout the year.

January. *Chinese New Year* is celebrated in Chinatown. (Sometimes falls in February.)

February. *Boston Festival*: winter festivities featuring ice-sculpting competitions. Often ties in with Valentine's Day celebrations.

March. *St. Patrick's Day*: Irish celebrations are particularly prominent in South Boston ("Southie"), the city's little Ireland.

April. *Patriot's Day*: re-enactments of the beginnings of the American War of Independence, focusing on Concord and Lexington. The *Boston Marathon* takes place on Patriot's Day (third Monday in April). One of the country's oldest sporting events, it now attracts over 9,000 participants.

May. *Boston Pops*: Boston Symphony Orchestra's two-month summer season begins. *Art Newbury Street*: open house for galleries, and jazz and classical music on the street (also in September). *Annual Kite Festival*: kite-making clinics and kite-flying in a festive atmosphere in Franklin Park. *Street Performers Festival*: magicians, jugglers and musicians take over Faneuil Hall Marketplace.

June. *Bunker Hill Day*: re-enactment of the battle and parade in Charlestown. *Boston Globe Jazz Festival*: a week of performances, including free midday concerts.

July. *Harborfest*: a week of concerts and special events (such as Chowderfest, a competition to find the city's best clam chowder, and the turnaround of the U.S.S. *Constitution*). Culminates with the *Boston Pops*' Fourth of July (Independence Day) concert and fireworks display on the Esplanade at the Hatch Memorial Shell. *Italian Street Festivals*: street parades, food, and entertainment most weekends in the North End (also in August). (See page 39)

October. *Columbus Day*: parade in East Boston or North End. *Head of the Charles Regatta*: enormous one-day rowing event.

December. *Boston Tea Party Re-enactment*: at both the Tea Party Museum and Old South Meeting House. *First Night*: city-wide New Year's Eve celebrations, with lively parades and firework displays.

From temporary exhibitions on Malcolm X to drama in converted buildings, Boston satisfies most.

You're never far from an **Irish pub**. One of the most atmospheric is the Black Rose, 160 State Street (behind Faneuil Hall Marketplace), with Guinness and nightly, live ballad music. At the Commonwealth Brewing Company, 138 Portland Street (near FleetCenter), they serve bitter, stout or porter. If the Bull and Finch (see page 28) on Beacon Hill is too busy, head for the Sevens, 77 Charles Street, a classic, friendly neighbourhood pub.

Outdoor Entertainment

In summer, the Boston Pops (see above) and various shows—film, dance, concert—take place at the Hatch Shell.

A band might take over the City Hall Plaza or Copley Square on Friday, when locals settle down for the evening with a deck chair. At any time of year, there's a medley of street entertainment, from saxophonists to Beatles singers, jugglers, fire eaters and much more around Harvard Square.

SPORTS

Spectator Sports

The **Red Sox** (baseball team) are much loved for their ever-so-close-to-winning tactics—they haven't quite pulled it off since 1918 when they last won a World Series. It's said that a curse has hung over the club ever since it traded Babe Ruth to the New York Yankees.

The **Celtics** (basketball) and the **Bruins** (ice hockey) are as victorious as the Red Sox are unsuccessful, with legendary players like the recently retired Larry Bird of the Celtics and Bobby Orr of the Bruins. The arena that witnessed their triumphs, Boston Graden, has been replaced by FleetCenter (see page 123 for ticket information).

Although the **Patriots** American football team play out of town at the Foxboro Stadium, every home game is usually sold out. The oldest annual marathon in the world—the **Boston Marathon**—is held on Patriot's Day (the third Monday in April), while the **Head of the Charles Regatta** takes place on the penultimate Sunday in October, with thousands of spectators lining the Charles River. (The marathon also attracts a huge audience.) Finally, sports fans should visit the New England Sports Museum (see page 67).

Participatory Sports

Boston Harbor is as busy as the city's streets, so you need to be extremely proficient if you want to sail. So long as you are, then pay a visit to the clubs situated on the wharves in Downtown.

Gentler sailing is possible on the Charles River. Contact Community Boating, behind the Hatch Memorial Shell on the Esplanade, tel. 523-1038. The expensive hotels have lap pools and gyms. The YMCA at 316 Huntington Avenue has extensive health facilities.

Put on your running shorts and jog along the Esplanade. If you want to have a go at the new rollerblading craze, you can hire equipment at Beacon Hill Skate, 135 Charles Street South, tel. 482-7400, as well as at Back Bay Bicycles,who can be found at 333 Newbury Street, tel. 247-2336. The traffic mayhem could easily put you off renting a bike.

CHILDREN

Parents are more likely to have a happy family holiday if they resist the temptation to regard a stay in Boston as one long history lesson. The best stops for children on the Freedom Trail are the U.S.S. *Constitution* and the detour to the Boston Tea Party Museum. On weekends, the National Historical Park and Boston by Foot (see page 114) lay on children's Freedom Trail walking tours.

Boston could hardly be better equipped with museums aimed at children; the Children's Museum, the Aquarium and the Museum of Science hold most children's (and parents') interest, while the Zoology Museum and Computer Museum in Cambridge appeal to young people.

At the Public Garden (see page 49) there is lots for younger children, with gentle rides on the swan boats in summer and the quaint *Make Way for Ducklings* statues:

If it all gets to be too much, climb aboard and escape to the coves and headlands of the coast.

Thrill to the lightning show at the Museum of Science.

Historic Neighborhoods (see page 114) manages to bring Robert McCloskey's tale to life. The zoo doesn't deserve a visit in its own right: combine it with other sights in the area. Much more exciting is a whale-watching trip (see page 47). Any harbour boat ride is a thrill; take a ferry to Boston Harbor Islands, where you can have a run-around and a swim.

Boston is a city tailor-made for sports-mad kids (not to mention parents). You'll find that at least one major league sports team is playing at any time of year. If you can't see the Bruins or Celtics in action, watch some of the greatest plays on video in the excellent New England Sports Museum (see page 67). Specialist shops all over town sell the teams' kits.

Find out what's on at the Puppet Showplace Theater in Brookline (tel. 731-6400). The *Boston Globe*'s weekly Calendar (see page 116) lists events for children and for teenagers, and the Convention and Visitors Bureau (see page 124) offers the useful *Kids Love Boston* guide and also provides a brochure which details hotels that have family accommodation rates.

EATING OUT

Boston offers a splendid culinary spread. With the Atlantic Ocean providing most of its ingredients, seafood afficionados will be in seventh heaven. By European standards, dining is very affordable.

When to Eat

As an alternative to a pricey hotel **breakfast**, try the many sit-down or take-out cafés located across the city. You will never be far away from an Au Bon Pain, a chain of French-style cafés that serves great coffee and a vast assortment of croissants and muffins.

Brunch is a leisurely affair, usually available from 1:00 A.M. to 3:00 P.M. on Sunday. Swanky hotels lay on gargantuan, eat-all-you-can buffets that will keep you going for the whole day.

A reflection of the city's fast pace of life is that many Bostonians eat **lunch** on the run, or grab a sandwich in a café. If you have lunch at a restaurant, you'll find that your meal costs considerably less than it would in the evening.

The leisured classes take **tea** between 3:00 P.M. and 5:00 P.M. Join them in the top hotels for a cup of Earl Grey and an irresistible tray of scones and cake.

Bostonians on the whole eat **dinner** early, typically somewhere between 6:30 P.M. and 9:00 P.M. A restaurant which is packed at 8:30 P.M. might be half-empty less than an hour later, so time your meals accordingly if you want to avoid a wait. However, it can be difficult to find somewhere to eat after 10:00 P.M.

Where to Eat

The diet of Beantown—as Boston is sometimes called—at one time consisted of beans, brown bread and boiled dinners. These days, you can only find those home-baked beans with the special sweet, smoky flavour in a few old-fashioned establishments, like Durgin-Park. More traditional Yankee dishes such as Indian pudding, can be found in other **landmark restaurants**, as ancient as the streets of the city itself. These include the Union Oyster House, Locke-Ober, and Parker's in the Omni Parker House hotel (consult our list of recommended establishments on pages 138–144 for more details).

In direct contrast, in the last decade a handful of ground-breaking chefs have dragged Boston's cuisine into the late 20th century. Try their wildly inventive **New England cuisine** at establishments such as Biba, Seasons, and Hammersley's Bistro. From a host of restaurants which specialize in **seafood**, the best known and most reliable is the successful Legal Sea Foods, with outlets around the city.

Ethnic restaurants are well represented throughout Boston too. You're spoilt for choice on Newbury Street, in the area around Faneuil Hall Marketplace, and also around Harvard Square in Cambridge.

For **fast food**, sandwiches are often "subs" (shaped like submarines) or "roll-ups," pitta bread made into a tube, with

Distinctly Continental! Relax over a coffee at a sidewalk café and watch the world go by.

many outlets satisfying pretzel and bagel cravings. It's worth braving the lunchtime scramble at Quincy Market in Faneuil Hall Marketplace for an amazing, mouth-watering conglomeration of food stalls.

Alternatively, indulge in a bit of **café life** on North End's Hanover Street, where in the morning you can sip cappucinos with characterful locals who have lived here for years, and in the evening eat *gelati* or *tiramisu* with Italian liqueurs. It's reckoned that Bostonians eat more ice cream per capita than people anywhere else in the U.S., so the chances are it'll never be far to an ice-cream store. See and be seen in the chic, *al fresco* coffee shops found along Newbury Street.

Scrod, Quahogs, and Lobster

Boston serves some of America's finest seafood—though a decline in local stocks and limits on catches mean much fish nowadays is actually imported into the region.

In a seafood restaurant, you can have virtually any type of **white fish**. The cheapest option is scrod—usually cod or haddock. Have it cooked any way you wish—broiled, fried, baked, grilled, Cajun, or pan-blackened—or try a **raw bar** (many restaurants have their own). Deft barmen shuck oysters and clams using a paring knife to slip open the shells, and diners sit at the bar slurping down the contents livened with lemon and tabasco.

If you're eating raw **clams**, they're likely to be hard shell or quahogs (*cohog*). The former are either cherrystones or littlenecks. Soft-shell clams, also called steamers, are an ingredient in clam chowder. The clam chowder in New England consists of clams, potatoes, and cream (Manhattan style, with tomatoes, is served elsewhere in the country)—a bowl can be a filling meal in itself.

Other delicacies like scallops, shrimps, and lobster are commonplace. If you've never tried **lobster**, now's the time. It's not saved for special occasions here: you can have a lobster pizza or sandwich, or raw lobster sashimi. Some restaurants offer Lazy Man's Lobster with the meat taken out, but that's missing the fun. Put on your bib and get to grips with your surgical implements.

Wining, dining, and socializing al fresco are quintessential summer pastimes in Boston.

Drinks

Bostonians are said to drink more beer than the inhabitants of any other city in the States. The local brew is a tasty lager called Samuel Adams. Restaurants often stock a good selection of California wines, and the wine lists at Italian and French restaurants offer labels from their native countries.

"Happy Hours"—when cut-price drinks are offered—are prohibited by the law of the state. Instead, many bars lure customers in with free buffet food early in the evening. You have to be over the age of 21 to drink legally in Massachusetts, and may be asked to produce photo identification with your date of birth on it (for example, a passport for non-U.S. citizens). For information on the best bars in town, see page 88.

INDEX

Where there is more than one set of references, the one in **bold** refers to the main entry. Page numbers in *italic* refer to an illustration.

HANDY TRAVEL TIPS

An A–Z Summary of Practical Information

Certain items of information in this section will be familiar to US residents, but have been included to assist overseas visitors.

ACCOMMODATIONS (See also CAMPING on page 107, YOUTH HOSTELS on page 128 and RECOMMENDED HOTELS on pages 130–137)

The Greater Boston Convention and Visitors Bureau (see TOURIST INFORMATION on page 124) can provide an up-to-date list of accommodations in the city (remember to add a 9.7 percent tax to the rates). It is always advisable to book ahead, especially in the July-August holiday season, and spring and fall, when conventions are in full swing.

Hotels. Boston hotels are relatively expensive, but of a high standard. Hotel and motel parking is usually available, but at a fee; the hotel bill may end up being considerably more than expected.

Bed & Breakfast. This is a good option to consider in Boston and a cheaper alternative to hotels. Few of the city's B&Bs take direct bookings; most use a reservations agency, and accept a booking for a minimum of two nights. Hosts are usually keen to please and some B&Bs are in period houses. Agencies thoroughly vet the B&Bs on their lists, ensuring good standards.

You may find somewhere to stay in the older residential parts of Boston, such as Beacon Hill or the South End, though many B&Bs are further out, in suburbs like Brookline. The owner usually has a daytime job, taking guests for extra income. The cost varies enormously, as does the level of comfort, privacy, and independence, and many B&Bs have a complete no-smoking policy. Try the following:

A B&B Agency of Boston, 47 Commercial Wharf, Boston, MA 02110; tel. 720-3540/1-800-CITY-BNB, fax 523-5761.

Bed & Breakfast Cambridge & Greater Boston, PO Box 665, Cambridge, MA 02140; tel. 576-1492/1-800-888-0178, fax 576-1430.

Host Homes of Boston, PO Box 117, Waban Branch, Boston, MA 02168; tel. (800) 600-1308 or 244-1308, fax 244-5156. (Publishes a list of its B&Bs.)

It would be a pity not to stay at least a night in one of the many beautiful, old-fashioned B&B inns on **Cape Cod** and the **North Shore**. Get a copy of the Massachusetts Bed & Breakfast Guide from the Massachusetts Office of Travel and Tourism (see TOURIST INFORMATION on page 124). For luxury B&B Inns on Cape Cod, you can also try:

DestiNNations, PO Box 1173, 15 C West Bay Road, Osterville, MA 02655; tel. (508) 428-5600/1-800-333-INNS, fax (508) 420-0565.

AIRPORTS

Logan International Airport is remarkably close to the city centre, just 5 km (3 miles) by road. (With the constant sight of planes swooping in over Boston Harbor, it feels even closer.) A big, busy national and international hub, it has five terminals, where you'll find information points, currency exchanges, duty-free shops, restaurants, and shops. Call **973-5500** for information.

A frequent shuttle bus service runs between the subway and terminals. Different shuttles serve different terminals, so be sure to get on the right one. For information on transportation to and from the airport, tel. **1 (800) 23-LOGAN**.

By far the cheapest and quickest way to get to and from the airport is by **subway** (see TRANSPORT on page 124). The journey from Government Center to the airport stop on the Blue Line takes about 10 minutes. The journey by **road** through the harbour tunnels can be subject to traffic jams, particularly at rush hour—a **taxi** ride from Downtown to the airport can take anything from 10 to 45 minutes. Delays add to the cost, making taxi-sharing common.

Minibus services run regularly from all major Back Bay and Downtown hotels. A regular **ferry** shuttle (Mon-Fri 6am-8pm; Sun noon-8pm) plies across Boston Harbor from Rowes Wharf, Downtown, and provides the most exciting way of arriving or departing. It takes seven minutes, connecting with a shuttle bus that circuits the terminals in 10 minutes, and it's free for children under 12.

CAMPING

Ask the Massachusetts Office of Travel and Tourism (see TOURIST INFORMATION on page 124) for a "Camping and Recreation in Massachusetts" leaflet, listing private and state campsites. The nearest to the city are on four of the Boston Harbor islands. They offer free "wilderness" camping—with no fresh water, for example. You need a permit; call Harbor Islands State Park, tel. 727-7676 for Lovells and Peddocks islands, and the Department of Environmental Management, tel. 740-1605, for Bumpkin and Grape islands.

CAR RENTAL/HIRE (See also DRIVING on page 111 and MONEY MATTERS on page 117)

Only consider renting a car if you want to make excursions.

To rent a car, you have to be over 21 years old (a surcharge may be made if you are under 25), and must show your driving licence. Visitors from non-English speaking countries may need a translation of their national driving licence as well as the original document itself. Agencies prefer credit card transactions (or demand a large cash deposit), and many will not rent a car to someone who does not have a major credit card unless they have a verifiable telephone listing and address in their own name.

Cars can be rented in Boston, Cambridge, and at Logan Airport, and you'll find agencies listed under "Automobile Renting and Leasing" in the Yellow Pages. For the main companies, car rental from the airport tends to be somewhat cheaper, but rates vary enormously from week to week and from company to company, so shop around—and don't forget to check about return facilities. (You may get the choice of returning the car with a full tank of petrol, or paying for a full tank in advance at a slightly reduced rate per gallon and then returning the car with an empty tank. Beware that if you don't make arrangements in advance, you may be charged an inflated rate to refill a tank.) Your insurance may provide all the coverage you need for a rental car, but if visiting from abroad, you should purchase a Collision Damage Waiver (CDW)—rates quoted exclude CDW.

A car booked from abroad will have some third-party liability insurance (check how much with your travel agent). When you pick up your car, the car-rental agency will offer extended third-party liability protection for an extra charge. Lastly, be sure to establish whether the rental agreement includes free unlimited mileage.

CLIMATE and CLOTHING

The weather in Boston is very varied and unreliable (a local saying: if you don't like the weather, wait a minute), though the changing seasons are part of the city's allure. Although it is normally cold and often snowy in winter, at times it can be mild. Spring usually passes quickly. Summer can be very hot and humid, with some occasional wet and chilly days, though the temperature tends to stay warm-to-hot with refreshing sea breezes.

Fall is famous in New England for the beautiful colours of the turning foliage. The time for this in Boston is mid-to-late October. Ask for a Fall Foliage Guide from the Massachusetts Office of Travel and Tourism (see TOURIST INFORMATION on page 124). There's even a Fall Foliage Hotline; call 727-3201. The chart below gives Boston's average minimum and maximum monthly temperatures:

		J	F	M	A	M	J	J	A	S	O	N	D
Max.	°F	36	37	43	54	66	75	80	78	71	62	49	40
Max.	°C	2	3	6	12	19	24	27	25	22	17	9	4
Min.	°F	20	21	28	38	49	58	63	62	55	46	35	25
Min.	°C	-7	-6	-2	3	9	14	17	17	13	8	2	-4

Clothing. Pack clothes to contend with the erratic weather. In winter, bring a warm coat, hat, gloves, and boots. In summer, tourist wear is a T-shirt and shorts, but bring a raincoat and sweater for cooler days, evenings, and boat trips. Though Boston is a laid-back city, in the evening people look casually smart, more so Downtown and in Back

Bay than in Cambridge. Most importantly, bring comfortable footwear: you'll probably be doing a lot of walking.

COMMUNICATIONS (See also TIME DIFFERENCES on page 123)

Post Offices. The United States Postal Service only deals with mail. Post office opening hours vary; most open Mon-Fri 8am-5pm, and Sat 9am-1pm. Hotels and shops also sell stamps, as do machines, but at a higher price than post offices. Collection times are marked on Boston's big mailboxes (blue with a red and white logo).

You can receive mail c/o General Mail Facility (poste restante), General Post Office, 25 Dorchester Ave., Boston, MA 02205; tel. 654-5225. It's located behind South Station.

Telephones. Information on rates, personal (person-to-person), reverse-charge (collect), and credit-card calls is given in the front of the White Pages of the directory. The area code for Boston is 617.

Operator	dial **0**
Local directory inquiries/area codes	dial **411**
Long distance inquiries	dial **1**, then **area code**, then **555-1212**
International dialling	dial **011**, then **country code**, then **area code**, then **phone number**
Emergencies	dial **911**

Calls are generally cheaper outside working hours (see OPENING HOURS on page 119). Making a call from a private phone is cheaper than from a public one, which in turn is less expensive than from a hotel-room phone. If you're phoning from your hotel room, check the rates first—you may find the public phone in the lobby more to your liking. Numbers with the prefix 800 (add the prefix 1 before the number) are free, but can only be dialled within the U.S.

Public phones take 5, 10 and 25 cent coins. For **local calls**, first deposit 10¢; wait for the dialling tone, then dial the seven-figure number. You may have to deposit more money, depending on the length of your call. For **long-distance calls**, dial the prefix 1, the three-digit area code, and the seven-digit number, and listen to the automatic voice for instructions on how much money to deposit. You may have to add extra during or after your call. For an **international call** to Europe, you have to deposit a large amount of change: the additional cost of a call from your hotel room may be worth it.

COMPLAINTS

If you feel you have a serious complaint to make about a business, and the manager of the establishment has not resolved the problem to your satisfaction, contact the Executive Office of Consumer Affairs and Business Regulation, 1 Ashburton Pl., Room 1411, Boston, MA 02108; tel. 727-7780.

CRIME (See also EMERGENCIES on page 113 and POLICE on page 121)

Boston feels relatively safe when compared to some other American cities. Here, everyone uses the subway and walks the well-lit streets until late at night.

However, you should visit certain areas—the Combat Zone, by Chinatown and the parks, the southern end of the South End, and parts of the southern suburbs—Roxbury and Jamaica Plain—only during daylight hours. You can reduce the risk of theft with a few precautions: always lock your hotel room and car (the state has a surprisingly high level of car crime); wear a minimum of conspicuous jewellery; and never leave bags and valuables unattended. In an emergency, phone **911**.

CUSTOMS and ENTRY FORMALITIES

Canadians only need provide evidence of their nationality. U.K. subjets no longer need a visa for stays of less than 90 days in the U.S., but do require a valid 10-year passport and a return airline ticket. The airline will issue a visa waiver form. Citizens of the Republic of Ireland, Australia, New Zealand and South Africa need a visa—check current information with your local U.S. consulate or embassy and allow up to three weeks for delivery.

Duty-free allowance. You will be asked to complete a customs declaration form before you arrive in the U.S. Restrictions are as follows, into: **USA** (if you are over 21): 200 cigarettes **or** 50 cigars **or** 2kg tobacco, 1 l of wine **or** spirits; **Australia**: 250 cigarettes **or** 250g tobacco, 1 l alcohol; **Canada**: 200 cigarettes **and** 50 cigars **and** 400g tobacco, 1.14 l wine **or** spirits **or** 8.5l beer; **New Zealand**: 200 cigarettes **or** 50 cigars **or** 250g tobacco, 4.5 l wine **or** beer **and** 1.1 l spirits; **Republic of Ireland**: 200 cigarettes **or** 50 cigars **or** 250g tobacco, 2 l wine **or** 1 l spirits; **South Africa**: 400 cigarettes **and** 50 cigars **and** 250g tobacco, 2 l wine **and** 1 l spirits; **U.K.**: 200 cigarettes **or** 50 cigars **or** 250g tobacco, 2 l wine **or** 1 l spirits.

For imports into the U.S., a non-resident may claim, free of duty and taxes, articles up to $100 for use as gifts, including an additional 100 cigars. Both arriving and departing passengers should report any money and cheques exceeding $10,000.

DRIVING

Driving in Boston is not a lot of fun. A local joke: don't use any signals as it gives away your strategy. If you arrive by car, put it in a garage until the end of your stay or until you want to take a trip out of town. Only hire a car if you want to go on excursions.

Driving conditions. Boston's road network is a haphazard mass of unnumbered, one-way streets which suffer from severe traffic congestion. It's a good idea to get a detailed city and state map and be clear about the number and direction of any freeway exits, as they can can come upon you with alarming speed. Take evasive action to avoid rush-hour driving near the city. In summer, if at all possible don't drive out to Cape Cod on a Friday night or back to Boston on a Sunday evening (the same advice applies, though less crucially, to travel to and from the North Shore).

Rules and regulations. Drive, of course, on the right; the speed limit is 88 km/h (55 mph) on highways, sometimes 105 km/h (65 mph) on turnpikes; always carry your driving licence; don't drink and drive. Rotaries (roundabouts) are common (give way to traffic already on the rotary); look out for signs telling traffic to give way to pedestrians; don't pass school buses (painted yellow) *in either direction* when passengers are getting off *or on* (indicated on the bus by flashing red signal lights). At traffic lights you can turn right on a red signal after stopping, unless a sign says to the contrary; on highways, traffic overtakes in both the inside and outside lanes. Finally, wearing seatbelts is compulsory in Massachusetts, whether you are in the front or back seats.

Tolls. Tolls are payable coming into Boston by bridge or tunnel from the north, and on the Massachusetts Turnpike. Keep a supply of quarters, dimes, and nickels available.

Gas (petrol). Some stations expect you to pay in advance, but in most you pay after you have filled up. Petrol from self-service pumps is cheaper than from service-assisted pumps.

Parking. It can be impossible to find on-street parking Downtown or in exclusive neighbourhoods such as Beacon Hill where virtually all spaces are for residents only. Establish in advance what parking facilities your hotel can offer (most hotels and smart restaurants have valet parking). There are a number of large underground parking lots throughout the city: ask the hotel concierge for details.

Breakdowns and accidents. The American Automobile Association (AAA) offers some breakdown assistance and touring information to members of affiliated organizations abroad. Contact the AAA at 1050 Hingham Street, Rockland, MA 02370 (tel. 871-5880). For the AAA emergency road service, phone 1 (800) AAA-HELP.

Road signs. Foreign visitors may be unfamiliar with the following two road signs.

Divided highway	Dual carriageway
Rotary	Roundabout

Fluid measures

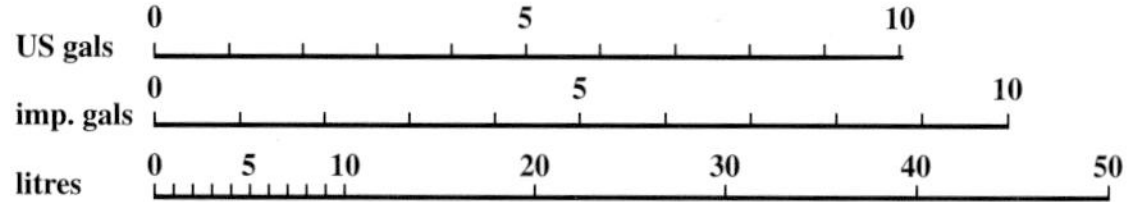

Distance

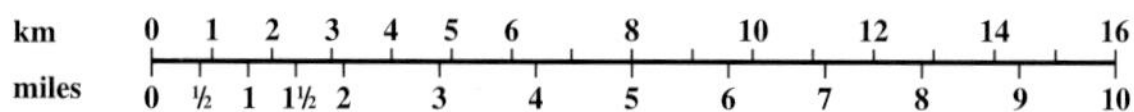

E

ELECTRICITY

The U.S. uses 110-volt 60-cycle AC. Plugs are small, flat and two-pronged. Visitors from overseas will need an adaptor.

EMBASSIES and CONSULATES

Australia: Suite 457, Statler Building, 20 Park Plaza, Boston, 02116; tel. 542-8655.

Canada: (Consulate) Suite 400, 3 Copley Place, Boston, MA 02116; tel. 262-3760.

Republic of Ireland: (Consulate) 535 Boylston St., Boston, MA 02116; tel. 267-9330.

South Africa: (Consulate) 333 East 38th St., 9th Floor, New York, NY 10016; tel. (212) 213-4880.

United Kingdom: (Consulate) Federal Reserve Plaza, 25th Floor, 600 Atlantic Ave., Boston, MA 022110; tel. 248-9555.

EMERGENCIES

(See also MEDICAL CARE on page 117 and POLICE on page 121)

Dial **911** and the operator will ask you if you want the police, an ambulance or the fire department. For a doctor, telephone **859 -1776.**

GAY and LESBIAN TRAVELLERS

Helpline: tel. 267-9001 (weekdays 4-11pm, weekends 6-11pm). For details of upcoming events and features, consult *In Publications*, New England's largest gay and lesbian newspaper, published weekly (258 Shawmut Avenue, Boston, MA 02118; tel. 426-8246).

GUIDES and TOURS

Trolley tours. After following the painted red line of the self-guided Freedom Trail (see page 25), the most popular way of seeing Boston is on a trolley tour. Old Town Trolley Tours (orange and green), Beantown Trolleys (red) and Boston Trolley Tours (blue) offer virtually identical 90-minute trips around Downtown Boston and its neighbourhoods. The narration depends on your guide, but you can always hop on and off. Booths selling tickets are liberally dotted throughout the city. Old Town Trolley Tours offer Cambridge tours too. For an unusual variation, try Boston Duck Tours, where the convertible "bus" plunges into the Charles River and becomes a boat at the end!

Walking tours. Rangers from the Boston National Historic Park (which covers the city's monuments) offer guided walks from the Visitor Center (see TOURIST INFORMATION on page 124). For the Black Heritage Trail, which is guided by a ranger and takes in the city's 19th-century African-American community around Beacon Hill, see page 24. Historic Neighborhoods (tel. 426-1885) and Boston by Foot (tel. 367-2345) have full programmes for exploring particular neighbourhoods. In Cambridge, Harvard students provide university tours from the Harvard Information Center, Holyoke Center, Massachusetts Avenue (tel. 495-1573). M.I.T. offers a similar service; visit the Information Office at 77 Massachusetts Avenue.

Excursions. As well as lengthy tours of Boston, Brush Hill Tours (tel. 236-2148) offers coach excursions to surrounding areas which include Lexington and Concord, Plymouth, Cape Cod, Salem and the North Shore.

Cruises. Companies offer harbour tours, trips further afield, sunset cruises, dinner cruises and whale watches (see page 47). **Boston Harbor Cruises**, Long Wharf (tel. 227-4321): harbour, sunset, whale-watch trips. Also water shuttle to Charlestown Naval Yard. **Bay State Cruise Company**, Long Wharf (tel. 723-7800): day trips to Provincetown (from Commonwealth Pier), whale watch, sunset, inner harbour, outer harbour, JFK Museum trips. Also ferry to Georges Island and a free inter-island service. **AC Cruise Line**, 290 Northern Ave. (tel. 261-6633). Toll-free call (800) 422-8419: day trips to Gloucester, whale watch.

Gourmet lunches and dinners on luxury craft are provided by Spirit of Boston, Rowes Wharf (tel. 457-1450) and Odyssey Cruises, Rowes Wharf (tel. 654-9700). **Whale watches** are also possible with Boston Harbor Whale Watch, Rowes Wharf (tel. 345-9866), and New England Aquarium Whale Watch, Central Wharf (tel. 973-5281). A 50-minute cruise up and down the **Charles** with Charles River Boat Company (tel. 621-3001), from CambridgeSide Galleria and the Museum of Science, is a pleasant, sedate experience.

L

LANGUAGE

Boston is full of pronounced accents, such as the smooth drawl of the upper classes and the rich resonances of the Irish tongue.

Most English-speaking foreigners are familiar with American words and phrases, but here are a few that may cause confusion.

U.S.	*British*
bill	banknote
check	bill (restaurant)
faucet	tap
first floor/2nd floor	ground floor/first floor
pants	trousers
purse/pocketbook	handbag

suspenders	braces
underpass	subway
undershirt	vest
vest	waistcoat

LOST PROPERTY

If you lose something on the MBTA, phone **722-3200**. If you lose something in a cab, call the Boston Police Department's Hackney Carriage Hotline on **536-8294**.

MEDIA

Radio and Television. AM and FM bands offer an unusual number of stations playing classical music. Every hotel room has a TV (B&Bs often don't), with network and a choice of cable channels. The main network channels are: channel 4 (CBS); channel 5 (ABC); channel 7 (NBC); channel 2 and 44 for PBS (Public Broadcasting Service) with no advertisements. Useful cable channels are CNN (Cable News Network) for non-stop news, the Weather Channel for national and local forecasts, MTV (Music TV), and ESPN for sports.

Newspapers and magazines. The city has two main papers, *The Boston Herald*, a meaty tabloid, and *The Boston Globe*, a serious broadsheet. Thursday's edition of *The Globe* has "The Calendar," an extensive listings section, while the "Night & Day" section on Sunday is more selective. *The Herald* has listings in its Friday edition.

There are several weeklies and fortnightlies. The most thorough, with reviews and listings, is the weekly *Boston Phoenix* (Friday). *The Improper Bostonian,* and *The Boston Tab* are good, with lots of suggestions for things to do. The free, monthly *Where Boston/Cambridge* magazine details shops, restaurants and entertainment. The monthly *Boston Magazine* is more critical, notably in its famous, fun, and influential Best and Worst annual review of all the city offers.

Out of Town News in Harvard Square, Cambridge, has a wide selection of publications from around the country and the world.

MEDICAL CARE (See also EMERGENCIES on page 113)

No vaccinations are required by U.S. health authorities, unless, of course, you are coming from known cholera or yellow fever areas.

The U.S. doesn't provide free medical services, and treatment is expensive. Overseas visitors should therefore make arrangements before leaving home (through a travel agent or an insurance company) for temporary health insurance with a high level of cover. Hospital emergency rooms will treat anyone in need of speedy attention.

Beth Israel Hospital: 330 Brookline Ave.; tel. 667-8000 (667-3337 for emergencies).
Cambridge City Hospital: 1493 Cambridge St.; tel. 498-1000.
Massachusetts General Hospital: 55 Fruit St.; tel. 726-2000.
Some medicines sold over the counter abroad are only available by prescription in the U.S.—check with your doctor. **CVS Drugstore**, 155 Charles St. (tel. 523-4372/523-1028) opens daily 8am-midnight.

MONEY MATTERS

Currency. The dollar is divided into 100 cents (¢). *Banknotes*: $1 (a buck), $5, $20, $50, $100. All notes are the same size and colour, so beware of mixing them up. *Coins*: 1¢ (penny), 5¢ (nickel), 10¢ (dime), 25¢ (quarter). 50¢ and $1 coins are rare.

Exchange facilities. Foreign visitors are advised to carry traveller's cheques and cash in dollars, and credit cards. It can be difficult to exchange foreign traveller's cheques and foreign currency for dollars. Visit outlets of Thomas Cook, Baybank, and Fleet Bank, as well as exchange kiosks at the airport.

Credit cards. Plastic is vital in making reservations and is the presumed method of payment for large transactions. Major credit cards are accepted almost everywhere, and can be used for drawing cash from cash machines (check with your bank for details).

Traveller's cheques. Traveller's cheques drawn on American banks are the easiest to use. Banks will exchange them for cash without a charge (take ID with you). Most establishments accept them directly as payment: $20 cheques are useful for such transactions. Change only small amounts at a time. Keep the balance of your cheques in the hotel safe and a note of their serial numbers in a separate place.

Tax. Advertised prices do not include tax. The Massachusetts State sales tax is 5.7 percent, levied on everything except medicine, food bought from a shop, and clothes under $175. Hotel tax is 9.7 percent.

PLANNING YOUR BUDGET

Here are some guideline prices of interest to visitors. Please note that prices vary greatly between one establishment and the next, and that inflation takes its toll.

Airport transfer. To and from Downtown, taxi $12-$18; minibus $7.50; ferry shuttle $8; subway 85¢.

Babysitters. $10-$15 an hour. Extra for more than 2 children. Minimum time 4 hours.

Bed & breakfast. $50-$140 for a double room.

Bicycle rental/hire. $20 a day.

Car rental/hire. Typical rate for a small car: $140 a week with unlimited mileage, plus $70-$80 a week for CDW (see DRIVING on page 111). However, the cost could be considerably higher or lower.

Entertainment. Cinema $7.50. Theatre $20-$90. Classical concert $10-$50. Comedy $5-$12. Nightclub $6-$15. Red Sox $7-$18. Bruins and Celtics $10-$50.

Gas (petrol). $1.05-$1.25 per U.S. gallon (approximately 4 litres) for regular unleaded at a self-service pump. Up to 20¢ extra if the pump is attended. Often more expensive at highway stations.

Hotels. Double room: budget under $100, moderate $100-$200, expensive $200 and up. Hotels often offer considerably lower rates than those they advertise; it's worth checking.

Laundry. In a laundromat $2 for wash and about $1.50 for drying; service wash for a load $10. Hotel service is around $2 a shirt.

Meals and drinks. Continental breakfast $2-$3; full breakfast $4-$10; lunch in a café $4-$6; lunch in a restaurant $8 and up; dinner $15 and up; fast-food meal $5; coffee $1-$1.50; beer $2-$4; glass of wine $3 and up; bottle of wine $12 and up; cocktail $4 and up.

Photography, video. Colour film (36 exposures) $6.50-$8; black and white film (36 exposures) $5. Blank video cassette $8-$10.

Public transport. MBTA pass $9 for 3 days, $18 for a week. Subway token 85¢. Local bus 60¢.

Rollerblade hire. $15 a day.

Taxis. $1.50 for first ¼ mile (150 meters), 20¢ for each subsequent ⅛-mile (75 meters).

Trolley tours. $10-$14.

Whale-watch trips. $16-$18.

OPENING HOURS (See also PUBLIC HOLIDAYS on page 121)

Banks: Mon-Fri 9am-3 or 4pm (or later), Sat 9am-noon or 2pm.

Museums, Galleries and Sights
(See also LEADING MUSEUMS AND GALLERIES on page 54)

Boston Tea Party Ship and Museum, Congress St. Bridge; tel. 338-1773. MBTA: South Station. Summer 9am-6pm; winter 9am-6pm; closed Dec-Mar 18. Adults $6.50, students $5.20, 5-14 years $3.25; children under 14 years $3.25, 5 years and under, free.

Bull and Finch Pub (known as *Cheers*), 84 Beacon St.; tel. 227-9605. MBTA: Arlington. 11am-2am. Free.

Bunker Hill Monument, Charlestown; tel. 242-5641. No.92 and 93 bus from Haymarket/MBTA: North Station. 9am-5pm. Free.

U.S.S. Constitution, Charlestown Navy Yard; tel. 242-5670. MBTA: North Station/ferry from Long Wharf. Daily 9.30am-3.50pm. For guided tours, 3.50pm to sunset for self-guided tours of the top deck. Free.

Constitution *Museum*, Charlestown Navy Yard; tel. 426-1812. Ferry from Long Wharf. Daily 9am-6pm in summer; daily 10am-5pm

Mar-May and Labor Day-Nov; 10am-3pm, Dec-Feb. Adults $4, seniors $3, 6–16 $2.

Faneuil Hall Marketplace. Faneuil Hall Square. MBTA: State/Park. Shops Mon-Sat 10am-9pm, Sun 12-6pm; restaurants and bars stay open later.

Faneuil Hall, Faneuil Hall, Marketplace; tel. 635-3105. 9am-5pm. Admission free.

John Hancock Observatory, Copley Square; tel. 572-6429. MBTA: Copley. Mon-Sat 9am-10pm, Sun, noon-10pm. Adults $3.75, 5-17 $2.25.

Longfellow National Historic Site, 105 Brattle St., Cambridge; tel. 876-4491. MBTA: Harvard Square. Daily tours 10.45am-4pm. $2 adults, seniors and all others free.

Massachusetts State House, Beacon St.; tel. 727-3676. MBTA: Park St., Mon-Fri, 10am-4pm. Tours free.

Old North Church, 193 Salem St.; tel. 523-6676. MBTA: Haymarket. Daily 9am-5pm. Free.

Old South Meeting House, Washington and Milk Streets; tel. 482-6439 MBTA: State. Summer daily 9.30am-5pm; winter Mon-Fri 10am-4pm, Sat-Sun 10am-5pm. Adults $2.50, students/seniors $2; 6-18 years $1; under 6 years free.

Old State House, State and Washington Streets; tel. 720-3290. MBTA: State. Daily 9.30am-5pm. Adults $3; students/seniors $2; children 6-18 years $1.50.

Paul Revere House, 19 North Square; tel. 523-2338. MBTA: Haymarket. Nov 1-April 14, 9.30am-4.15 pm; April 15-Oct 31, 9.30 am - 5.15 pm. Adults $2.50; Students and seniors $2; 5-17 years $1; under 5 years free.

Sports Museum of New England, CambridgeSide Galleria; tel. 57-SPORT. MBTA: Science Park/Lechmere. Mon-Sat 10am-9.30pm, Sun 11am-7pm. Adults/over 11 $6, 4-11/seniors $4.50.

Restaurants: many stop serving food as early as 10pm.

Shops: Mon-Sat 9 or 10am-5.30 or 7pm, Sun some noon-5 or 6pm. Shopping malls may stay open Mon-Fri until 9 or 9.30pm, and on Sunday afternoons.

P

PHOTOGRAPHY and VIDEO

Drugstores/chemists and supermarkets sell film at lower prices than specialist camera shops. Airport X-ray machines do not usually affect ordinary film; ask for hand inspection of high-speed film. Video tape is available for all cameras. Pre-recorded tapes bought in the U.S. do not run on European video players (and vice versa), and tape conversion is usually expensive.

Boston's fickle weather poses the greatest challenges for photographers, but seasonal changes—snow, blossom, the fall colours—offer the greatest rewards. The city is safe enough to carry expensive camera and camcorder equipment out on the streets.

POLICE

In an emergency, phone **911**. Police, wearing dark blue, are generally very approachable. Their presence is very visible—on foot, horseback, bicycle, motorbike, and in cars. They also patrol the MBTA.

PUBLIC HOLIDAYS

Banks, businesses and some stores are closed on the following days (except where otherwise indicated).

January 1	*New Year's Day*
Third Monday in January*	*Martin Luther King Day*
Third Monday in February*	*Presidents Day*
Third Monday in April**	*Patriots Day*
Last Monday in May	*Memorial Day*
July 4	*Independence Day*
First Monday in September	*Labor Day*
Second Monday in October*	*Columbus Day*
November 11*	*Veterans Day*

Fourth Thursday in November	*Thanksgiving Day*
December 25*	*Christmas Day*

*shops open
** some shops and businesses open; banks open am

RELIGION

Many different denominations are found in Boston, and the city is also the world centre for the Christian Science movement (see page 52).

Hotels can provide details of church and synagogue services. The Yellow Pages list places of worship under "Churches." Also, the Saturday newspapers give information on Sunday services (see page 116).

TICKETS

The Greater Boston Convention and Visitors Bureau compiles a seasonal travel planner which gives dates, names of shows and phone numbers for all main music, dance, theatre, and sports events/venues. Use the hotel concierge service for assistance. The agencies listed on the next page can provide tickets, where available, for most events.

Bostix Booth (Tues-Sat 10am-6pm, Sun 11am-4pm; tel. 723-5181), at Faneuil Hall and Copley Square, may offer half-price tickets for same-day performances.

In Cambridge, visit **Out of Town Tickets** (Mon-Fri 9am-7pm, Sat 9am-11pm; tel. 492-1900), in the subway area under Harvard Square. Cash and major credit cards in person; credit card bookings over the phone.

For credit card bookings, contact **Concertcharge**, tel. 497-1118; or **Ticketmaster**, tel. 931-2000.

For baseball, basketball and hockey games, try to buy tickets as far in advance as your travel planning allows. Some standing room or general admission tickets are available for all games on the day.

Baseball: *Boston Red Sox*, Fenway Park, Yawkey Way; tel. 267-1700. From April to October.

Basketball: *Boston Celtics*, FleetCenter; tel. 624-1820. From November to April.

Football: *New England Patriots*, Foxboro Stadium, Foxboro; tel. 1(800) 543-1776. 40 km (25 miles) south of Boston. Special trains from South Station, Back Bay Station. Tickets are usually easily obtainable. From September to December.

Hockey: *Boston Bruins*, FleetCenter; tel. 624-1820. From October to April.

TIME DIFFERENCES

Continental U.S. has four time zones: Boston is on Eastern Standard Time. From April to October, Daylight Saving Time is adopted and clocks move ahead one hour. The chart below shows winter times.

Los Angeles	**Boston**	London	Johannesburg	Sydney
9am	**noon**	5pm	7pm	4am

TIPPING

Waiters and waitresses earn most of their salary from tips (often they are paid little else) and in restaurants, the check (bill) hardly ever includes service. In cafés where you pay the cashier on the way out, the tip should be left on the table. In a bar, you're expected to leave the change from buying a drink on the bar top and tip as you would in a restaurant for table service. Some suggestions:

Tour guide	10-15%
Hairdresser/barber	15%
Hotel porter (per bag)	\$1-\$1.50
Taxi driver	15-20%
Waiter/waitress	15-20%

TOURIST INFORMATION

Greater Boston Convention and Visitors Bureau, Prudential Tower, PO Box 490, Boston, MA 02199; tel. 536-4100/1(800) 888-5515, provides *The Official Guidebook*, *Travel Planner,* and *Kids Love Boston* brochure, and the *Family Friendly Hotel Packages and Special Discounts* leaflet. A new service, "Boston by phone," is a 24-hour line which links callers from North America directly to suppliers in seven fields of interest to the tourist. Phone **1 (800) 374-7400**.

Massachusetts Office of Travel and Tourism, 100 Cambridge St., 13th Floor, Boston, MA 02202; tel. 727-3201, publishes guides for accommodation, bed & breakfast, attractions, events and the Fall Foliage Guide (see CLIMATE on page 108).

Visitor Information Center, in a booth on the Tremont St. side of Boston Common, and in the Prudential Center. Mon-Fri 8.30am-5pm, Sun 9am-5pm.

National Park Service Visitor Center, 15 State St.; tel. 242-5642, is open Mon-Fri 8am-5pm, Sat-Sun 9am-5pm; summer 6pm. It's the best place for information on historical sights. Also at Charlestown Naval Yard; tel. 242-5601. Open 9am-5pm (summer 6pm).

Cambridge Discovery Inc, in the centre of Harvard Square (tel.497-1630), is open Mon-Sat 9am-6pm, Sun 1-5pm.

For **general information** on travel in the U.S., contact the United States Travel and Tourism Administration in your own country.

TRANSPORT (See also CAR RENTAL on page 107, DRIVING on page 111, and TRAVELLING TO BOSTON on page 126)

The Massachusetts Bay Transportation Authority (MBTA), also called the "T," runs subway trains, trolleys, buses and commuter trains throughout the city and beyond. For further information, call 222-3200/1-800-392-6100. A subway and bus visitor pass, called the Boston Passport, allows unlimited travel on buses or subways in Boston (1-day $5, 3-days $9, 7-days $18). They can be purchased from the Visitor Information Center on Boston Common daily from 9am to 5pm. Maps and information are available from the Park St. station. Children between five and eleven travel half price, under-fives for free.

Subway. (See also the MBTA map on the cover of this guide.) The MBTA (Massachusetts Bay Transportation Authority) runs the subway (the country's oldest, dating from the 1890s). It's a safe and reliable system of underground and overground trains and trolleys. There are four lines—red, green, blue and orange—with trains coloured to match. Stops are marked on the street by the letter T in a circle. If you have a pass you're just waved through; otherwise, buy a token from the booth and deposit it or the exact amount in change in the turnstile at the start of your journey. Platforms are marked "Inbound" – meaning that the train is going in the direction of Park Street or Downtown Crossing—or "Outbound." Note that the red and green lines have branches: letters on the front of trains correspond to the branch destinations. Trains start running at 5am (a little later on Sundays), and the last ones leave Downtown around 12:45am.

Bus. Buses run on cross-town routes and to outer suburbs (details on the Metro Boston Transit Map). Exact change is required on buses.

Train. Commuter Rail, also known as the Purple Line, is useful for visitors primarily for getting out to the North Shore (on the so-called Beach Train) and to places inland like Concord. There are three city-centre stations: North Station (for trains to Concord and the North Shore), South Station, and Back Bay. In all three, you will find maps showing the whole network, and schedules for individual lines.

Taxi. Travelling by taxi is expensive, and because of Boston's traffic, not always the quickest way of getting from A to B. There are several competing firms. Most taxis wait in lines outside hotels and in shopping and dining centres like Downtown Crossing and Faneuil Hall Marketplace. If you want to go to somewhere off the beaten track, don't rely on the driver knowing where it is.

Here are a few names and phone numbers: **Checker**: 536-7000 (Boston)/497-1500 (Cambridge); **Red and White Cab**: 242-0800; **Town Taxi**: 536-5000.

TRAVELLERS WITH DISABILITIES

The Information Center for Individuals with Disabilities, 29 Stanhope St., 4th floor, P. O. Box 256, Boston, MA 02210-1606 (tel. 1-800-462-5015; telecommunications device for the deaf 345-9743) offers written advice on access to hotels, restaurants, sights and transport. Very Special Arts Massachusetts, The China Trade Center, 2 Boylston St., 2nd Floor, Boston, MA 02116 (tel. 350-7713) publishes *The Access Expressed!* directory. An inexpensive booklet by Charles Bahne, *The Complete Guide to Boston's Freedom Trail*, gives details of wheelchair access at each site.

TRAVELLING TO BOSTON

From the United States and Canada

By air. Direct flights operate from all main U.S. cities to Boston. Major airlines run shuttle services from Chicago and New York, and there are frequent direct flights from Montreal and Toronto.

By bus. Greyhound links Boston to all major centres in North America, with hourly departures to Washington, New York, and Montreal. Tel. 1-800-231-2222. Foreign travellers can purchase an Ameripass (it must be bought outside the U.S.) for unlimited travel within a set period. Phone the Greyhound representative in your own country.

By rail. Boston is the terminus of Amtrak's Northeast Corridor route from Washington, Philadelphia, New York, and the east end of the Lake Shore Limited route from Chicago. Packages which include accommodations are available. For information in the U.S. and Canada, call 1-800-USA-RAIL. Amtrak has representatives in all major countries. Rail passes for unlimited travel within a set period are offered to foreigners: the Coastal and Eastern Rail Pass covers Boston.

From abroad. Air fares are usually much more expensive in summer and at Christmas. An Apex fare or equivalent is often the cheapest, but restricts you to a minimum stay of 7-14 nights and must be purchased a certain length of time in advance (the longer ahead you book, the lower the fare). Standbys are increasingly becoming a thing of the past.

From the UK. Major airlines fly direct daily from Gatwick and Heathrow (non-stop London-Boston takes roughly 7 hours). Contact "bucket shops" advertised in local papers for cheap consolidated fares. There is also a direct service from Glasgow.

From the Republic of Ireland. There are direct flights from Dublin (with one touch-down); the journey takes approximately 9 hours. Otherwise, transit via London.

From Australia and New Zealand. Airlines fly via San Francisco or Los Angeles from Sydney, Melbourne, and Auckland. Flying time from Melbourne is roughly 19 hours; from Auckland 17 hours 15 min (with stops along the way).

From South Africa. There is a wide choice of indirect flights via Europe (usually London), Miami or New York. Flying time from Johannesburg to Boston is 18 hours 20 min (with stops along the way).

Packages. Some airlines and major tour operators offer all-inclusive flight and accommodation "city breaks." These sometimes work out cheaper than paying for an air fare and a hotel room separately.

Airpasses. Travellers from abroad who may make **domestic flights** within the U.S. could save considerably by buying an air pass before reaching the country. These are offered by most major U.S. airlines.

WEIGHTS and MEASURES (See also DRIVING on page 111)

The U.S. is one of the last countries in the world to adopt the metric system, and has not yet started an official changeover programme. For U.K. tourists, the main difference between British and American measures is: 1 U.S. gallon = 0.833 British Imperial gallon = 3.8 litres.

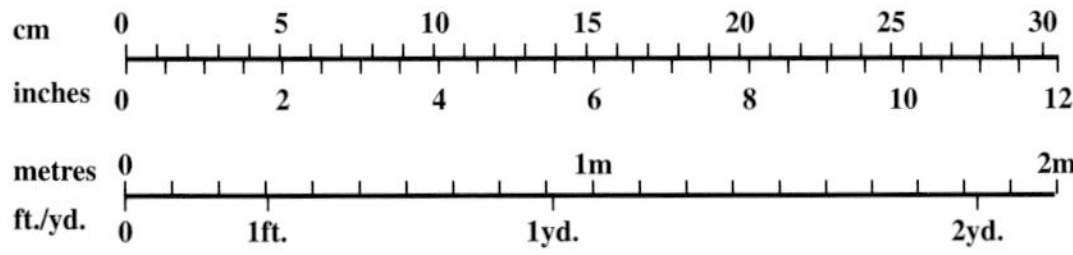

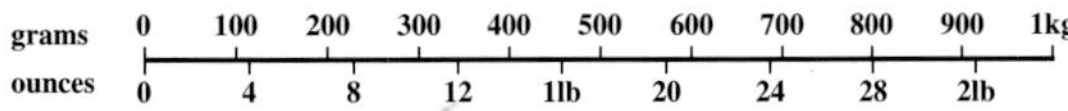

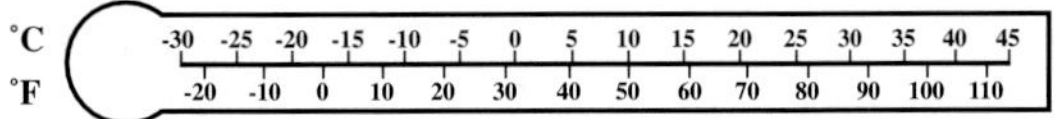

YOUTH HOSTELS

For the cheapest accommodations ($15-18 per night), try Boston International AYH-Hostel, 12 Hemenway St., Boston, MA 02115; tel. 536-9455. Membership, available on the spot, is required in summer. More information from Greater Boston Council AYH, 1020 Commonwealth Ave., Boston, MA 02215; tel. 731-5430/731-6692.

YMCAs and YWCAs are more comfortable: $50-56 double, $35-39 single. For men and women: YMCA, 316 Huntington Ave., Boston, MA 02115; tel. 536-7800 (pool and health club). For women: YWCA, 40 Berkeley St., Boston 02116; tel. 482-8850.

A SELECTION OF HOTELS AND RESTAURANTS

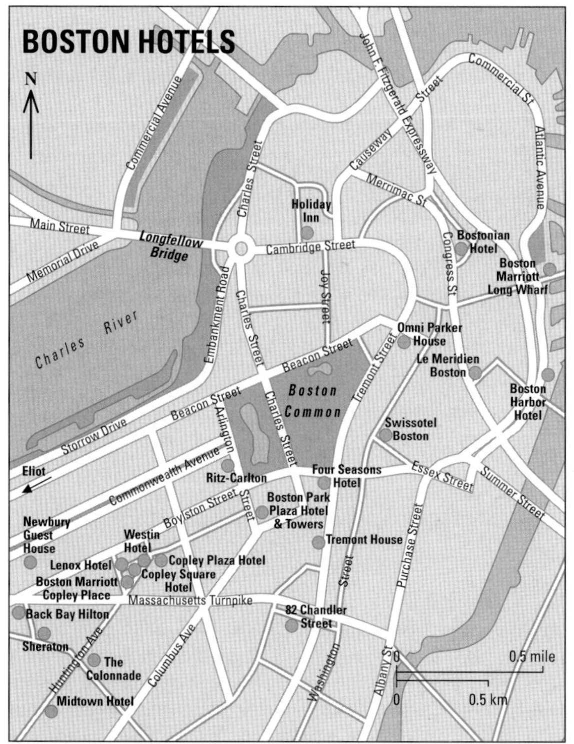

Recommended Hotels

Although accommodations in Boston are relatively expensive (for cheaper lodging, try Bed & Breakfast or youth hostels—see ACCOMMODATIONS on page 105 and YOUTH HOSTELS on page 128), they're also of a high standard, both in the new chain hotels and in the various lovingly restored landmark buildings. Bedrooms are usually fully equipped, including individual temperature controls, direct-dial phones, cable TV and quite often much more, and nearly every hotel in the city has a concierge desk for dealing with guests' whims or queries.

Be sure to book ahead in case your stay collides with a convention, when it can be very difficult to find a room in the city. Almost all hotels have a U.S. toll-free "1-800" phone number.

The price bands below serve as a guideline for the cost of a standard double room per night (for two people), excluding tax (9.7 percent) and breakfast. Single rates are usually about 10 percent less, and often you can have an extra bed in the room for a small charge. Many hotels do not charge for children staying in their parents' room. Though there is little seasonal variation in cost, many hotels have much lower weekend rates or family rates: ask when making your reservation.

✪✪✪✪	above $250
✪✪✪	$175-250
✪✪	$125-175
✪	below $125

BEACON HILL

Holiday Inn Government Center ✪✪ *5 Blossom Street, Boston, MA 02114; Tel. (617) 742-7630; Toll-free 1-800-HOLIDAY; Fax (617)* 742-4192. Situated very close to Beacon Hill, near the Charles River, and is a convenient stop for Faneuil

Hall Marketplace. The hotel has recently been refurbished and offers good quality bedrooms, most of which enjoy views of the city. Sweeping views are also part of the attraction of the top floor cocktail lounge—the perfect place to relax with an evening drink. Outdoor pool. 303 rooms.

DOWNTOWN

Regal Bostonian Hotel ✪✪✪ *Faneuil Hall Marketplace, Boston, MA 02109; Tel. (617) 523-3600; Toll-free 1-800-343-0922; Fax (617) 523-2454.* The only Boston hotel by Faneuil Hall Marketplace, and one of the smallest luxury hotels in the city. Small and swanky, part modern (in the Bostonian wing) and part converted 19th-century warehouse (in the Harkness wing). Restaurant, bar, 153 rooms. (See also page 139.)

Le Meridien Boston ✪✪✪ *250 Franklin Street, Boston, MA 02110; Tel. (617) 451-1900; Toll-free 1-800-543-4300; Fax (617) 423-2844.* Good value weekend rates for this financial district hotel housed in the old Federal Reserve Bank. The bedrooms are in over 150 different styles. 326 rooms. (See also page 139.)

Omni Parker House ✪✪✪ *60 School Street, Boston, MA 02108; Tel. (617) 227-8600; Toll-free 1-800-THE-OMNI; Fax (617) 742-5729.* The longest-operating hotel in the U.S., situated in central Downtown, has housed many famous guests and staff over the years. Historic bar and restaurant. Some of the bedrooms are small and plain for the price however. 538 rooms.

Swissôtel Boston ✪✪✪ *1 Avenue de Lafayette, Boston, MA 02111; Tel. (617) 451-2600; Toll-free 1-800-621-9200; Fax (617) 451-0054.* Business-oriented, 22-floor tower block situated at the rough end of Downtown Boston. Tasteful interior with antique and modern furnishings. Smart bedrooms, pool, well-equipped health club. Rates include breakfast. 497 rooms.

THEATER DISTRICT

Tremont House ✪✪ *275 Tremont Street, Boston, MA 02116-5694; Tel (617) 426-1400; Toll-free 1-800-331-9998; Fax (617)*

482-6730. Good value, theatre-district hotel (ask about complimentary theatre tickets) housed in a building that was once the headquarters for the Benevolent Protective Order of the Elks. Recently refurbished; marble columns and glittering chandeliers recall past days. Two dance clubs. 290 rooms.

WATERFRONT

Boston Harbor Hotel ✪✪✪-✪✪✪✪ *70 Rowes Wharf, Boston, MA 02110; Tel. (617) 439-7000; Toll-free 1-800-752-7077; Fax (617) 330-9450.* This is Boston's luxurious waterfront hotel, set in a dazzling modern wharf building, with an airport ferry service to its doors. Pleasantly informal, with the city's best hotel health club. 230 rooms.

Boston Marriott Long Wharf ✪✪✪ *296 State Street, Boston, MA 02109; Tel. (617) 227-0800; Toll-free 1-800-228-9290; Fax (617) 227-2867.* Atrium hotel in a harbourside setting. Modern rooms: request one with a harbour view. 400 rooms.

BACK BAY

Back Bay Hilton ✪✪✪ *40 Dalton Street, Boston, MA 02115; Tel. (617) 236-1100; Toll-free 1-800-874-0663; Fax (617) 267-8893.* Small (by Boston standards) Back Bay chain hotel in a triangular-shaped tower. The establishment prides itself on offering its guests peace and quiet. 335 rooms.

Boston Marriott Copley Place ✪✪-✪✪✪ *110 Huntington Avenue, Boston, MA 02116; Tel. (617) 236-5800; Toll-free 1-800-228-9290; Fax (617) 236-5885.* A massive, modern hotel in the Copley Place complex in the heart of Back Bay. A wide variety of dining options is available off the stylish, frenetic atrium, and a mall with 100 shops is attached to the lobby. Good health centre with pool, and golf and tennis are available nearby. 1,147 rooms.

Boston Park Plaza Hotel and Towers ✪✪-✪✪✪✪ *64 Arlington Street, Boston, MA 02116-3912, Tel. (617) 426-2000; Toll-free 1-800-225-2008; Fax (617) 426-5545.* Constantly busy but nonetheless efficient, offering shops, bars, and restaurants, all housed in a 1927 building. Conveniently positioned in a central location near the Public Garden. Family-run, it's known for an enlightened environmental programme (water-saving shower heads, dispenser systems for bathroom shampoos and soaps, a team of "Green Staff" examining methods of minimizing waste and recycling). 977 rooms.

Colonnade Hotel ✪✪✪ *120 Huntington Avenue, Boston, MA 02116; Tel. (617) 424-7000; Toll-free 1-800-962-3030; Fax (617) 424-1717.* A relatively small and peaceful alternative to its Back Bay chain-hotel neighbours. Stylish and elegant, this is somewhere that prides itself on the fact that no detail is too small to be overlooked, from employing staff who speak several languages to the selection of toiletries in the bathroom. Modern, comfortable, with a roof pool and a jazz bar. 288 rooms.

Copley Plaza Hotel ✪✪✪ *138 St. James Avenue, Boston, MA 02116; Tel. (617) 267-5300; Toll-free 1-800-996-3426; Fax (617) 267-7668.* Boston's *grand dame* is a 1912 showcase hotel on Copley Square, frequented by the city's elite: dazzling public rooms with glittering chandeliers, mirrors and marble, and comfortable bedrooms with tasteful decor and quality reproduction furniture. 370 rooms.

Copley Square Hotel ✪ *47 Huntington Avenue, Boston, MA 02116; Tel. (617) 536-9000; Toll-free 1-800-225-7062; Fax (617) 267-3547.* Good value, cosy Back Bay hotel which has been in operation since 1891, and is now benefiting from a recent refurbishment. Some of the bedrooms are on the small side, but have good facilities. Fun, popular bar—the Original Sports Saloon. 143 rooms. (See also page 141.)

Eliot Hotel ✪✪✪ *370 Commonwealth Avenue, Boston, MA 02215, Tel. (617) 267-1607; Toll-free 1-800-44-ELIOT; Fax (617) 536-9114* . Kitchenettes, period furnishings, and marble bathrooms distinguish this elegant, mainly suite hotel in the outskirts of Back Bay. No public rooms, but nonetheless good value. 92 rooms.

Four Seasons Hotel ✪✪✪✪ *200 Boylston Street, Boston, MA 02116; Tel. (617) 338-4400; Toll-free 1-800-332-3442; Fax*

(617) 423-0154. Boston's finest hotel is a relaxed celebrity haunt overlooking the Public Garden. Superb service and housekeeping. Popular piano bar and an impeccable health club with a wide range of facilities. Try the acclaimed Aujourd'hui restaurant (see page 141). 288 rooms.

Lenox Hotel ✪✪ *710 Boylston Street at Copley Place, Boston, MA 02116; Tel. (617) 536-5300; Toll-free 1-800-225-7676; Fax (617) 266-7905.* The Lenox is an ideally placed, small, old-fashioned Back Bay hotel with a touch of class. The rooms are comfortable and decorated in a variety of styles. There are 212 rooms.

Midtown Hotel ✪ *220 Huntington Avenue, Boston, MA 02115; Tel. (617) 262-1000; Toll-free 1-800-343-1177; Fax (617) 262-8739.* Simple, spacious rooms are offered in this motel-style building on the edge of Back Bay. Outdoor pool. 159 rooms.

Newbury Guest House ✪✪ *261 Newbury Street, Boston, MA 02116; Tel. (617) 437-7666.* Book weeks in advance for this prime-located Bed & Breakfast: a lovely Victorian building in the heart of Back Bay, beautifully furnished with antiques. 32 rooms.

Ritz-Carlton Boston ✪✪✪✪ *15 Arlington Street, Boston, MA 02117; Tel. (617) 536-5700; Toll-free 1-800-241-3333; Fax (617) 536-1335.* Next to the Public Garden, coiffeured doormen, white-gloved elevator operators and strict dress codes characterize Boston's most distinguished hotel. Here the café, bar, lounge, and dining-room are all institutions in their own right. The Old Wing bedrooms are the more desirable. 278 rooms.

Sheraton Hotel and Towers ✪✪✪ *39 Dalton Street, Boston, MA 02199; Tel. (617) 236-2000; Toll-free 1-800-325-3535; Fax (617) 236-1702.* Part of the Prudential Center, it is two hotels in one, with the standard Sheraton below and the luxurious Towers on the top floors, where guests have their own butler. The best features of the lower hotel are the well-equipped rooms, a large outdoor pool, a seafood restaurant, and an American diner. 1,208 rooms in total.

Westin Hotel ✪✪✪ *Copley Place, 10 Huntington Avenue, Boston, MA 02116; Tel. (617) 262-9600; Toll-free 1-800-228-*

3000; Fax (617) 424-7483. A 36-storey tower block overlooking a large lobby, with a choice of dining (three restaurants, including Turner Fisheries, see page 142, and three bars). Connected to Copley Place shopping centre. 800 rooms.

THE SOUTH END

82 Chandler Street Bed & Breakfast ✪ *82 Chandler Street, Boston, MA 02116; Tel. (617) 482-0408; Toll-free 1 (888) 482-0408.* A beautifully furnished, no-smoking B&B. 3 rooms, each with private bath; complimentary family-style breakfast.

CAMBRIDGE

Cambridge House Bed & Breakfast Inn ✪ *2218 Massachusetts Avenue, Cambridge, MA 02140-1836; Tel. (617) 491-6300; Toll-free 1-800-232-9989; Fax (617) 868-2848.* Lovely, restored, clapboard house with elaborate but warm bedrooms in Victorian style, many with four-poster beds. Worthwhile, despite its poor main road location in the Cambridge suburbs (a short walk to the subway). 14 rooms.

Charles Hotel in Harvard Square ✪✪✪ *1 Bennett Street, Cambridge, MA 02138; Tel. (617) 864-1200; Toll-free 1-800-882-1818; Fax (617) 864-5715.* An oasis of peace and luxury in the centre of Cambridge. Stylishly modern, with attentive staff, chic bedrooms and a highly rated jazz club. Good-value weekend packages are sometimes available. 296 rooms.

Harvard Square Hotel ✪✪ *110 Mount Auburn Street, Cambridge, MA 02138; Tel. (617) 864-5200; Toll-free 1-800-458-5886; Fax (617) 864-2409.* A no-frills modern hotel, with recently renovated public and guest rooms; well run and just a few steps from Harvard Square centre. 72 rooms.

The Inn at Harvard ✪✪ *1201 Massachusetts Avenue, Cambridge, MA 02138; Tel. (617) 491-2222; Toll-free 1-800-222-8733; Fax (617) 491-6520.* Across from Harvard Yard; books and art are scattered liberally in this new but traditionally styled hotel, built around a four-storey atrium. 113 rooms.

Royal Sonesta Hotel Boston ✪✪-✪✪✪ *5 Cambridge Parkway, Cambridge, MA 02142; Tel. (617) 491-3600; Toll-free 1-800-SONESTA; Fax (617) 661-5956.* Smart riverside complex near the CambridgeSide Galleria. Rooms with river views cost more, but are worth it. 400 rooms.

CONCORD

Colonial Inn ✪-✪✪ *48 Monument Square, Concord, MA 01742; Tel. (978) 369-9200; Toll-free 1-800-370-9200; Fax (978) 369-2170.* Attractive building, dating back, in parts, to 1716 and set right in the centre of town. Low ceilings and wide beams, antique furniture and quilts, and air conditioning in the newer part of the Inn.

Hawthorne Inn ✪ *462 Lexington Road, Concord, MA 01742; Tel. (978) 369-5610; Fax. (978) 287-4949.* An 1870s house lying east of Concord centre. 7 rooms.

PLYMOUTH

John Carver Inn ✪ *25 Summer Street, Plymouth, MA 02360; Tel. (508) 746-7100; Toll-free 1-800-274-1620.* A professionally run hotel in colonial-style near the centre of Plymouth. Well-equipped bedrooms are offered, as well as a good-value restaurant with lots of character. Outdoor pool. 79 rooms.

Pilgrim Sands Motel ✪ *150 Warren Street (Route 3A), Plymouth, MA 02360; Tel. (508) 747-0900; Toll-free 1 (800) 729-SANDS; Fax. (508) 746-8066.* Situated close to Plimoth Plantation, this motel has all the usual facilities, plus an indoor-outdoor pool and some rooms with ocean views. 64 rooms.

CAPE COD

Captain Freeman Inn ✪-✪✪ *15 Breakwater Road, Brewster, MA 02631; Tel. (508) 896-7481; Fax (508) 896-5618; Toll-free 1-800-843-4664.* A comfortable hotel in an elegant Victorian home belonging to a sea captain, furnished with four-poster beds. Outdoor pool. A little pedantically run. 12 rooms.

Watermark Inn ✪✪ *603 Commercial Street, Provincetown, MA 02657; Tel. (508) 487-0165; Toll-free 1-800-734-0165; Fax (508) 487-2383.* One of the most pleasant places to stay in Provincetown. Ocean views and beautiful sunsets from the 10 suites, all equipped with kitchenettes.

Whalewalk Inn ✪-✪✪ *220 Bridge Road, Eastham, MA 02642; Tel. (508) 255-0617; Fax (508) 240-0017.* One of the Cape's most civilized, welcoming inns, the Whalewalk was built in the 1830s as a whale master's home. Offers a very peaceful atmosphere. Not always easy to locate, so ask for directions in Eastham. 12 rooms.

SALEM

Amelia Payson House ✪ *16 Winter Street, Salem, MA 01970; Tel. (508) 744-8304.* This lovely bed and breakfast inn was renovated by the owners in the 1980s. Rooms have brass or four-poster beds. The inn is just a short walk from the Witch Museum and all Salem's attractions. 4 rooms.

Hawthorne Hotel ✪ *Salem Common, Salem, MA 019070; Tel. (508) 744-4080; Toll-free 1-800-SAY-STAY; Fax (508) 745-9842.* The most central hotel in Salem, and the largest, though it has a cosy feel. Some of the rooms overlook Salem Common. 89 rooms.

CAPE ANN

Addison Choate Inn ✪-✪✪ *49 Broadway, Rockport, MA 01966; Tel. (508) 546-7543; Toll-free 1-800 245-7543; Fax (508) 546-7638.* Rooms are beautifully furnished with antiques. Two, large self-contained apartments in the Carriage House. Outdoor pool. Short walk from town centre. 8 rooms.

Inn on Cove Hill ✪ *37 Mount Pleasant Street, Rockport, MA 01966; Tel. (508) 546-2701.* Some rooms are small, but all are immaculately furnished. Narrow spiral staircase leads to upper floors. Short walk from town centre. 11 rooms, 9 with bath.

Recommended Restaurants

Bostonians dine out en masse, so be sure to reserve a table in advance wherever possible. This will also enable you to check that the restaurant is open: some establishments are open for dinner only, and close one or two nights a week. Some of the best-known places have a no-reservations policy, so stoical hour-long waits are often necessary. A delay can usually be softened by a drink at the bar—you may find that you can eat here too, taking your pick from the full restaurant menu or from an enticing selection of appetizers.

As in the rest of the U.S., portions tend to be generous (don't be shy about asking to take away what you cannot eat). Light eaters may find that two courses or just an entrée (main course) generally suffices. Although Boston is becoming less formal than it once was, some long-established dining-rooms still operate a policy of jacket and tie.

The price bands below indicate the cost of a three-course dinner, excluding drinks, tax (5 percent) and tips (15 to 20 percent expected). Lunch is almost always considerably cheaper than an evening meal, and many restaurants offer bargain dining in "early bird" specials (typically before 7pm).

✪✪✪ above $40

✪✪ $20-$40

✪ under $20

BEACON HILL

Hungry i ✪✪ *7½ Charles Street; Tel. (617) 227-3524.* Housed in a tiny Charles Street basement, this intimate restaurant with red brick walls and patterned china serves contemporary American cuisine with rich sauces and delicious European desserts.

Rebecca's ✪✪ *21 Charles Street; Tel. (617) 742-9747.* Sandwiches, brunch menus and dinners in a fashionable bistro.

Ristorante Toscano ✪✪-✪✪✪ *41-47 Charles Street; Tel. (617) 723-4090.* A civilized and tasteful Florentine restaurant that prides itself on the authenticity of its cuisine. Book well in advance.

DOWNTOWN

Blue Diner ✪ *150 Kneeland Street (at South Street, near Financial District); Tel. (617) 338-4639.* Old-fashioned diner with sophisticated touches. Substantial entrées with mashed potatoes and vegetables, and home-made cake. Open 24 hours, seven days a week.

Durgin Park ✪-✪✪ *340 North Market Street, Faneuil Hall Marketplace; Tel. (617) 227-2038.* A 130-year-old institution famed for its belligerent staff and home-made baked beans. Yankee cooking served at communal tables.

Julien ✪✪✪ *Le Meridien Hotel, 250 Franklin Street, (Financial District); Tel. (617) 451-1900 Ext. 7120.* French *haute cuisine* in opulent surroundings. Book in advance.

Locke-Ober ✪✪✪ *3 Winter Place (in the Downtown Crossing); Tel. (617) 542-1340.* A club-like, brahmin stronghold since 1875—women were only admitted to the Men's Café two decades ago. Carved wood and stained glass, jacket and tie, and classic traditional American and European dishes.

Seasons ✪✪✪ *Regal Bostonian Hotel, Faneuil Hall Marketplace, corner of North and Blackstone streets; Tel. (617) 523-4119.* Luxurious, modern oasis looking over Faneuil Hall Marketplace. State-of-the-art, New American cuisine and seasonally changing menus. Book ahead.

Union Oyster House ✪✪ *41 Union Street (near Government Center); Tel. (617) 227-2750.* Boston's oldest restaurant, established in 1826, is—according to many—one of the best and most atmospheric shellfish bars in town. Plenty of New England seafood to choose from.

THEATER DISTRICT

Brew Moon ✪ *115 Stuart Street; Tel. (617) 523-6467.* A modernistic microbrewery, Brew Moon offers American food, a trendy atmosphere, and several homemade beers. You can dine outdoors in fine weather.

Jacob Wirth ✪-✪✪ *31 Stuart Street; Tel. (617) 338-8586.* German dishes such as sauerkraut, wiener schnitzel, and a comprehensive choice of beers in a bar-cum-restaurant that has retained its original 19th-century fittings.

THE NORTH END

Daily Catch ✪✪ *323 Hanover Street; Tel. (617) 523-8567.* This restaurant offers first-rate Sicilian seafood. Tiny, fun, casual, and always packed. Also at 261 Northern Avenue (at Fish Pier), Waterfront; tel. (617) 338-3093.

European ✪ *218 Hanover Street; Tel. (617) 523-3989.* Boston's oldest Italian restaurant. Cavernous and uninspiring to look at, it serves huge great pizzas and lots of seafood.

Mamma Maria's Ristorante ✪✪ *3 North Square; Tel. (617) 523-0077.* Above average Italian cuisine is served in this stunning little upstairs restaurant on North Square. Black and white decor dominates the intimate dining rooms.

Ristorante Lucia ✪✪ *415 Hanover Street; Tel. (617) 367-2353.* Intense, serious but informal Italian restaurant. Its extensive menu offers traditional and adventurous dishes. Over-the-top murals decor.

WATERFRONT

Anthony's Pier 4 ✪✪✪ *140 Northern Avenue; Tel. (617) 423-6363.* A famous seafood restaurant, with fabulous Harbor views, that has fed everyone from Liz Taylor to George Bush. Book ahead.

No Name Restaurant ✪ *15½ Fish Pier (off Northern Avenue next to the World Trade Center); Tel. (617) 423-*

2705. A no-frills, lots-of-fun establishment providing cheap, top-quality seafood. Popular with tourists—expect a wait.

BACK BAY

Atlantic Fish Co. ✪✪ *777 Boylston Street; Tel. (617) 267-4000.* Informal restaurant with a wide-ranging menu and a raw bar.

Aujourd'hui ✪✪✪ *Four Seasons Hotel, 200 Boylston Street; Tel. (617) 351-2071.* Very exclusive and plush restaurant overlooking the Public Garden, with soft furnishings and oil paintings. Excellent seasonal cuisine. Reservations recommended.

Biba ✪✪-✪✪✪ *272 Boylston Street (at Arlington Street); Tel. (617) 426-7878.* Inventive New American cuisine and bold decor in a favourite upmarket, informal restaurant. Meals are also served at the trendy bar. Reservations essential.

Café Budapest ✪✪✪ *Copley Square Hotel, 90 Exeter Street; Tel. (617) 734-3388.* Hungarian cuisine in bizarre, old-fashioned basement dining-rooms. Said to be Boston's most romantic restaurant. Book ahead.

Davio's ✪✪-✪✪✪ *269 Newbury Street (at Gloucester Street and Fairfield Street); Tel. (617) 262-4810.* One of the street's most popular haunts: northern Italian cuisine in a formal dining-room (reservation required) and an al fresco café.

L'Espalier ✪✪✪ *30 Gloucester Street (at Newbury Street); Tel. (617) 262-3023.* Arguably the best French restaurant in town, in a Victorian townhouse. Very expensive, with very formal service. Book ahead.

Gyuhama ✪✪ *827 Boylston Street (at Gloucester Street); Tel. (617) 437-0188.* A Japanese restaurant serving (meticulously) the best sushi in town. Very popular with Japanese and non-Japanese alike.

Hard Rock Café ✪ *131 Clarendon Street (at Stuart Street); Tel. (617) 424-7625.* Decent hamburger fare amid rock memorabilia, blaring music and crowds. Good for the kids.

Legal Sea Foods ✪✪ *35 Columbus Avenue; Tel. (617) 426-4444.* The continuously frenetic flagship restaurant of a famous chain. Impeccably fresh, cleanly presented seafood cooked any which way you want. An unmissable Boston experience, but expect a wait. Popular branches also located at Copley Place, 100 Huntington Avenue, Back Bay; tel. (617) 266-7775, as well as in Cambridge at Kendall Square, 5 Cambridge Center; tel. (617) 864-3400.

The Ritz-Carlton Boston Dining Room ✪✪✪ *Ritz-Carlton Boston Hotel, 15 Arlington Street; Tel. (617) 536-5700.* Tried and tested traditional French cuisine and New England specialities in sumptuous surroundings of chandeliers, drapes, and a lavish, gold ceiling. Reservations strongly recommended.

Turner Fisheries ✪✪ *Westin Hotel, Copley Place, 10 Huntington Avenue; Tel. (617) 424-7425.* Top-notch straightforward seafood and probably the city's best chowder, in somewhat antiseptic modern surroundings. There's also a raw bar and a jazz bar.

THE SOUTH END

Botolph's on Tremont ✪ *569 Tremont Street (at Clarendon Street); Tel. (617) 424-8577.* Fine and out-of-the-ordinary Italian Cuisine. Delicious pasta and pizza concoctions are presented among modern art and hip South Enders. Good value.

Hammersley's Bistro ✪✪-✪✪✪ *553 Tremont Street; Tel. (617) 423-2700.* Some of the city's best New England and French country cuisine in a casual, trendy ambience.

CHINATOWN

Chau Chow ✪ *52 Beach Street; Tel. (617) 426-6266.* Serves superb Chinese food, especially seafood, to regular locals and non-Chinese alike. Across the street is the larger Grand Chau Chow, open until 4:00 A.M.

CAMBRIDGE

Border Café ✪ *32 Church Street, Harvard Square; Tel. (617) 864-6100.* This Tex-Mex restaurant is one of Cambridge's busiest young hangouts. Expect a long wait, and look forward to plain wooden tables, murals and margaritas.

Casablanca ✪-✪✪ *Brattle Theater, 40 Brattle Street, Harvard Square; Tel. (617) 876-0999.* An upscale bar (with a mural of Rick's Café) and restaurant, with bluesy music and a mix of pizza, pasta, burgers and Moroccan food.

Dali ✪✪ *415 Washington Street (at Beacon Street), Somerville; Tel. (617) 661-3254.* Out-of-the-way, authentic and joyful Spanish restaurant, known for its tapas in particular.

East Coast Grill ✪✪ *1271 Cambridge Street (at Prospect Street), Inman Square. Tel. (617) 491-6568.* Superb barbecue and spicy Caribbean food, washed down with daiquiris and margaritas in a noisy, cramped and extremely busy dining room. Expect a long wait.

Harvest ✪✪ *44 Brattle Street, Harvard Square; Tel. (617) 492-1115.* New American concoctions in a boldly designed bistro with a romantic terrace. Serves both affordable eats and expensive dinners.

Rialto ✪✪✪ *Charles Hotel, 1 Bennett Street, Harvard Square, Cambridge; Tel. (617) 661-5050.* This restaurant offers the most exciting hotel dining in Cambridge with its marvellous southern Mediterranean menu.

Upstairs at the Pudding ✪✪✪ *10 Holyoke Street, Harvard Square; Tel. (617) 864-1933.* Unique restaurant in an airy room and with a gorgeous roof terrace, above the Hasty Pudding Theater. Excellent northern Italian and European fare. Book ahead.

PLYMOUTH

The Lobster Hut ✪ *Town Wharf, Plymouth; Tel. (508) 746-2270.* A "fast seafood" eatery, the Lobster Hut offers great, cheap seafood dinners at outdoor picnic tables overlooking the harbour.

CAPE COD

Aesop's Tables ✪✪✪ *Main Street, Wellfleet; Tel. (508) 349-6450.* A fine restaurant specializing in New American dishes, which are served in no fewer than six different dining rooms in a traditional summer mansion. Open from mid-May to mid-October. Reservations strongly recommended.

Impudent Oyster ✪-✪✪ *15 Chatham Bars Avenue, Chatham; Tel. (508) 945-3545.* Varied meals served in a boisterous atmosphere.

Lobster Pot ✪✪ *321 Commercial Street, Provincetown; Tel. (508) 487-0842.* Fresh, simply prepared seafood served in a relaxing setting, overlooking the beach. Find out what the lunchtime specials are—they are often good value. No reservations.

Napi's ✪-✪✪ *7 Freeman Street, Provincetown; Tel. (508) 487-1145.* An eclectic interior is complemented by an extensive menu and tasty food at Napi's. This is the best restaurant in Provincetown for vegetarians. Unfortunately, it is only open for dinner in summer; better to come in winter when it serves three meals a day.

SALEM

Nathaniel's ✪✪ *Hawthorne Hotel, Salem Common; Tel. (508) 825-4311.* Nathaniel's offers the finest beef, seafood, and poultry dishes in a refined setting.

CAPE ANN

Folly Cove Pier Restaurant ✪-✪✪ *325 Granite Street,, Rockport; Tel. (508) 546-6568.* A great place for lobster and other seafood. Open in summer only.

Peg Leg Restaurant ✪✪✪ *18 Beach Street, Rockport; Tel. (508) 546-3038.* A good choice for either lunch or dinner, when you can choose from lobster, seafood, and tasty specialities such as scallop pie.